Fun & Fancy
Jackets & Vests

℮

Fun & Fancy Jackets & Vests

Folk Art Using No-Sew Appliqué

❧ Patrick Lose ❧

Sterling Publishing Co., Inc.   New York
A STERLING/CHAPELLE BOOK

Assistant to Patrick Lose: Lenny Houts

For Chapelle:

Owner: Jo Packham

Editor: Cathy Sexton

Staff: Sandra Anderson, Trice Boerens, Rebecca Christensen, Holly Fuller, Sharon Ganske, Cherie Hanson, Holly Hollingsworth, Susan Jorgensen, Susan Laws, Amanda McPeck, Jamie Pierce, Leslie Ridenour, Nancy Whitley, and Lorrie Young

Photography: Ryne Hazen and
                 Kevin Dilley for
                 Hazen Photography

Models: Kay Ballif, Trina Bates, Lisa Christensen, Amy Dawson, Valerie Kimball, Becky LaRose, and Aimee Martinez

All original illustrations in this book are by Patrick Lose. If you would like more information about Patrick's designs and "Out on a Whim" patterns for wearable art, quilts, wood and holiday crafts, write to: Out on a Whim, P.O. Box 400, Van Meter, Iowa 50261.

For more information on where to purchase full-size patterns in this book, write to: Customer Service Department, Chapelle Designers, P.O. Box 9252, Ogden, Utah 84409.

Library of Congress Cataloging-in-Publication Data

Lose, Patrick.
        Fun & fancy jackets & vests : folk art using no-sew appliqué / Patrick Lose.
                p.   cm.
        Includes index.
        ISBN 0-8069-1298-7
        1. Appliqué—Patterns. 2. Wearable art. 3. Vests. 4. Coats.
    I. Title. II. Title: Fun and fancy jackets and vests.
    TT779.L67 1995
    746.44'50432—dc20   95-6
                                                               CIP

10 9 8 7 6 5 4 3 2 1

Published by Sterling Publishing Company, Inc.
387 Park Avenue South, New York, NY 10016
© 1995 by Chapelle Ltd.
Distributed in Canada by Sterling Publishing
c/o Canadian Manda Group, One Atlantic Avenue, Suite 105
Toronto, Ontario, Canada M6K 3E7
Distributed in Great Britain and Europe by Cassell PLC
Wellington House, 125 Strand, London WC2R 0BB, England
Distributed in Australia by Capricorn Link (Australia) Pty Ltd.
P.O. Box 6651, Baulkham Hills, Business Centre, NSW 2153, Australia
Printed and Bound in Hong Kong
All Rights Reserved

Sterling ISBN 0-8069-1298-7

*This book
is dedicated to
Mom and Dad
for their
love and support
in my
unconventional pursuits!*

Appliqué refers to the process of creating pictures with fabric. There are several ways to accomplish this. One method is machine stitched appliqué. In this process, a decorative machine stitch, such as a satin stitch or blanket stitch, is used to permanently affix the fabric elements of the picture to the background fabric. In this case, a jacket or vest. No seam allowances are used on the appliqué motifs. When using a satin stitch, the raw edges of these pieces are covered by the decorative stitching. When using a looser stitch, such as the blanket stitch, the raw edges are still visible and create a more "primitive" look.

No-Sew Appliqué is simply what the term implies. By using fusible adhesive (HeatnBond is the brand used in the projects throughout this book) and an iron, these fabric elements are quickly, and easily, applied to the garment. Raw edges are finished and embellished using dimensional paint. See General Instructions: Dimensional Paint and No-Sew Appliqué on page 9. Although the No-Sew method of appliqué can be used on the projects designed for this book, all appliqué projects but the Jolly Jack-o-Lantern vest (photo on page 58) were created using the machine stitched appliqué method. If you choose the No-Sew method of appliqué, refer to the General Instructions: Dimensional Paint and No-Sew Appliqué on page 9 and simply replace satin stitching with dimensional paint.

Regardless of the method of appliqué you choose, we know that you will enjoy creating the jackets and vests that are featured in this book.

CONTENTS

GENERAL INSTRUCTIONS

Abbreviations:
>   RST = right sides together
>   WST = wrong sides together
> $^5/_8$" seam allowance unless otherwise noted
> $^3/_8$" seams used for binding

Appliqué Patterns:
Using tracing paper and a fine-point black marker, you can transfer all appliqué patterns that have been included in this book. To transfer appliqué patterns to the HeatnBond, the tracing paper should be flipped over and the HeatnBond placed on top, paper side up. Trace all pattern pieces on the solid outer line to the HeatnBond. Broken lines are for positioning and/or painting lines.

Basting:
Basting stitches are temporary stitches done by hand or machine to hold layers of fabric in place.

Bias Strips:
Fabric, when cut at a 45-degree angle to its grain, is called bias. The term often refers to pieces cut in strips and sewn together for the purpose of binding a raw edge. To cut bias strips, fold the fabric at a 45-degree angle to the grain of the fabric and crease. Cut strips the width indicated in the instructions and parallel to the crease. The ends of the bias strips should be on the grain of the fabric. RST, piece strips by mitering ends as shown in Diagram A below. Continue to piece the strips until they are the length that is called for in the instructions.

JOINING BIAS STRIPS

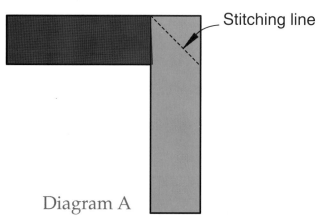

Stitching line

Diagram A

Buttons and Buttonholes:

To mark button positions, WST, match right and left fronts of garment opening. Push a pin through the outer end of the buttonhole and through the button side of the garment. At this point, mark the buttonhole position with a non-permanent marking pen. When sewing buttons, use a thread approximately 36" long. Fold the thread in half and thread the folded point through the eye of the needle. This will give you a double strand. With this double strand, you don't need to make as many stitches. Always knot thread securely on the inside of the garment.

Buttonholes should always be properly spaced and marked before they are stitched. Mark the top and the bottom buttonholes and divide the distance between these two points into the desired number of buttonholes. The projects with buttons in this book are designed to have horizontal buttonholes. If you are using a $3/4$" button, the first buttonhole should be positioned $3/4$" down from the neck edge and $3/4$" in from the right jacket/vest front edge. Follow the same rule with other size buttons, but realize that the pattern you are using has been drafted with a specific size button required. You may have to make pattern adjustments if you wish to use another button size. You may also add more buttons if desired. Buttonholes can be stitched by hand or by machine.

Clipping Curves and Trimming Corners:

Seam allowances on corners, curves, or points should be clipped to create ease and reduce bulk. Clip into the seam allowance at approximately $1/4$" intervals, cutting to, but not through, the stitching.

Covering Buttons:

A button cover kit comes with all the tools needed to cover buttons. To cover buttons, refer to the manufacturer's instructions provided with the brand chosen.

Dimensional Paint and No-Sew Appliqué:

Dimensional paint can be used in the same way satin stitching is used to cover the raw fabric edges in appliqué. Embellish as desired with additional painted lines. Use a steady hand and pressure on the bottle. Any stray paint splatters can easily be removed with a straight pin or a toothpick.

Dry flat for four (4) to six (6) hours. The paint will cure completely in 24 hours and the garment can be washed in 72 hours. To launder, turn inside out and wash in warm water on a delicate cycle. Tumble dry on low heat. Dry cleaning is not recommended when dimensional paints are used.

When using dimensional paints, carefully follow manufacturer's instructions.

Embroidery Stitches:

Buttonhole Stitch:

Buttonhole stitches create a distinct pattern and are especially effective on edges. There they serve as a tool for outlining as well.

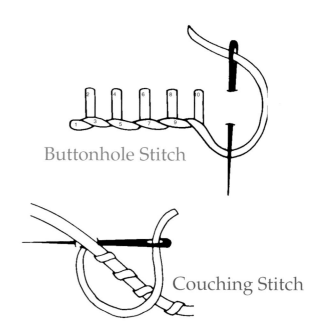

Buttonhole Stitch

Couching Stitch:

Couching offers a nicely curved line where back-stitching may be too angular. Couching is also an attractive way to anchor a heavier floss, metallic thread, or ribbon.

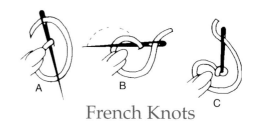

Couching Stitch

French Knots:

French knots are used to make facial features such as eyes and noses. In a large scene, the smallest flowers may be French knots, or French knots may be the repeated accent of a border.

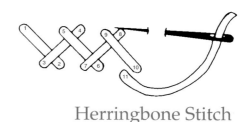

French Knots

Herringbone Stitch:

Herringbone stitches are easy to make perfectly on even-weave fabrics by simply counting threads. The herringbone stitch is a pleasing pattern for a border design.

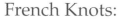

Herringbone Stitch

Lazy Daisy Stitch:

Lazy daisy stitches are most often used for flowers and leaves.

Lazy Daisy Stitch

Satin Stitch:

Satin stitches offer a smooth, shiny surface that creates a change of texture.

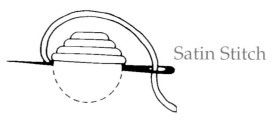

Satin Stitch

Enlarging Project Patterns:

Patterns that are too large for the pages in this book are prepared on a grid in which each square is equal to one inch (1") on the finished pattern. To enlarge a pattern, select a piece of tracing paper large enough to accommodate the finished size of the pattern. Mark grid lines one-inch (1") apart to fill the paper. Begin marking dots on the one-inch (1") grid lines where the reduced pattern intersects the corresponding grid lines. Connect the dots.

A product made for this purpose is available in fabric stores. It has dots printed on it at 1" intervals. One-inch (1") graph paper can also be used.

Transfer all information such as "place on fold." All patterns in this book include a $^5/_8$" seam allowance for construction and a $^3/_8$" seam allowance for binding.

Notches:

Some pattern pieces are marked with small notches. Match the notched edges to align the pieces correctly.

Piecing Bias Strips and Binding:

Bias strips of fabric, pieced together end-to-end with a mitered seam, are used to bind the raw edges of the garments in this book.

To bind the jacket/vest, press one long side of the pieced binding one-half inch ($^1/_2$") to the wrong side. Beginning at one of the side seams on the lower edge of the jacket/vest, place the binding strip on the vest, RST, aligning the raw edge of the jacket/vest with the long, unfolded raw edge of the binding. Fold over one-half inch ($^1/_2$") at the beginning of the binding. Stitch the binding around the jacket/vest, through all layers, using a $^3/_8$" seam allowance and mitering all corners (see "Note" on page 12).

When you get all the way around the jacket/vest, overlap the binding strips one-half inch ($^1/_2$") beyond the fold where you started. Trim off any excess binding and clip all curves.

Turn the other long folded edge of the binding strip over the raw edge of the garment to the inside. Place the folded edge slightly over the stitching line created when the binding was sewn to the garment. Pin binding securely in place and stitch by hand or machine, being sure to catch the edge of the binding on the inside. If machine stitching, you can either top-stitch close to the folded edge on the outside of the garment, or you can stitch "in the ditch" (seam) of the binding on the outside. If you stitch in the ditch, we recommend using invisible thread in the needle and a bobbin thread that matches the inside fabric. All raw edges of the jacket/vest are bound in the same manner, including the armholes or sleeve hems.

Piecing Bias Strips and Binding (Continued):

Note: To miter corners, stop stitching $3/8$" from the corner, then back-stitch. Fold the binding on a diagonal fold as shown in Diagram A. Hold in place while folding the binding back down as in Diagram B. Pin in place so that the raw edge of the binding now aligns with the raw edge of the next side of the jacket/vest. Resume stitching the next side, as shown in Diagram B. Finish stitching around the jacket/vest repeating this process on all corners.

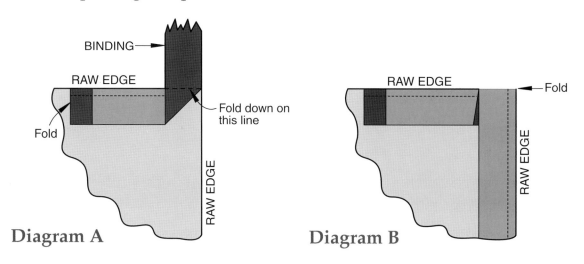

Diagram A   Diagram B

Raw Edge:

The unfinished edge, usually cut with scissors, is sometimes called a raw edge.

Sizing:

The following chart is a guide to the sizes used when these patterns were created. We have made every effort to include patterns that will fit most body shapes and sizes. It is important that you select a size that is slightly on the large side so that you can allow for any alterations. Please measure and fit carefully. Note that all patterns do not have the XS and XXL sizes.

Sizing	Bust	Waist
X-Small	$30^1/_2$-$31^1/_2$"	23-24"
Small	$32^1/_2$-34"	25-$26^1/_2$"
Medium	36-38"	28-30"
Large	40-42"	32-34"
X-Large	44-46"	37-39"
XX-Large	48"	40"

Satin Stitching by Machine:

Machine satin stitching is done with a very close zigzag stitch setting. Satin stitching is used to appliqué and cover raw fabric edges. Practice, using several different stitch lengths and widths, until desired look is achieved.

Satin Stitching by Machine (Continued):

When you are satin stitching a line that is not crossed with another line of satin stitching, start by putting the needle of the machine into the fabric. Pull the thread underneath the foot toward you. Lower the foot and begin stitching over the thread. When you reach the end, cut thread, leaving enough to thread through a hand needle. Push the point of the needle under a few rows of stitches and down through all layers to the back of the piece. Knot this thread on the back and snip off the excess. This will keep the satin stitching from coming undone.

Seam Allowance:

The space between the stitched seam and the raw edge of the fabric is known as the seam allowance. All patterns in this book include a $^5/_8$" seam allowance for construction and a $^3/_8$" seam allowance for binding. Any exceptions are noted in specific project instructions. Seam allowances of curved seams should be clipped to create ease. Corner seam allowances should be trimmed to reduce bulk.

Vermicelli Stitching:

Use invisible thread for top-stitching and thread that matches the lining in the bobbin. With a scrap of cotton batting sandwiched between the vest fabric and lining, test the stitch before starting on the vest. You do this stitch with the feed dogs on your machine lowered. Beginning somewhere in the center of the piece, start stitching in a free-form manner. You will follow an imaginary line that looks like a "vermicelli" noodle on a plate, but it never crosses over itself. As the "noodle" curls around and around, randomly from the center to the outside of your piece, each curve line stays $^1/_4$" to $^1/_2$" away from the one next to it. Continue to stitch on the sample until you are comfortable with this "freehand" stitching.

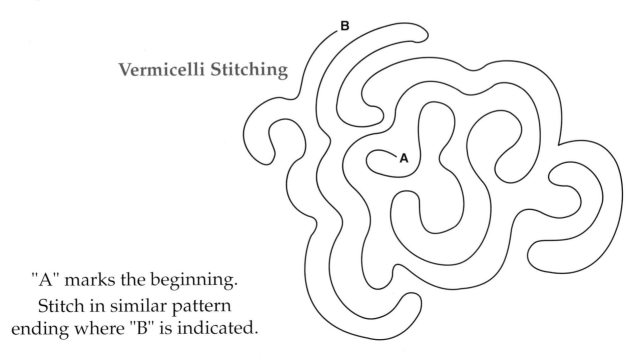

Vermicelli Stitching

"A" marks the beginning.
Stitch in similar pattern
ending where "B" is indicated.

Playing
with
Patches

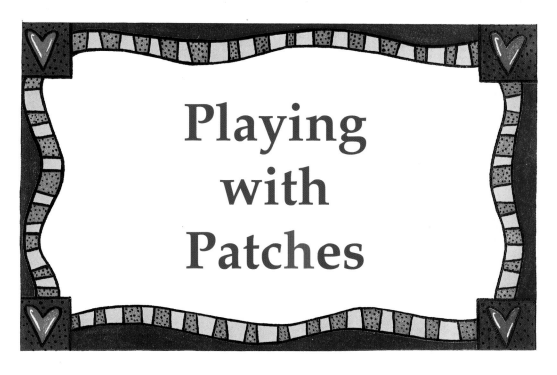

Playing with Patches

Use "Vest B" patterns — see pages 124-125.
All fabrics are 100% cotton.

Materials

	XS	S	M	L	XL
Lining — 45" wide	$7/8$ yd.	1 yd.	$1^1/4$ yds.	$1^1/4$ yds.	$1^1/3$ yds.
Muslin Underlining — 45" wide	$7/8$ yd.	1 yd.	$1^1/4$ yds.	$1^1/4$ yds.	$1^1/3$ yds.

For all sizes:

- Fabric 1: $1/2$ yard — we used navy with hearts and stars
- Fabric 2: 1 yard — we used ivory
- Fabric 3: $1/4$ yard — we used red and blue checkered print
- Straight and bias binding: 1 yard of deep red fabric
- Fusible knit interfacing: $1^1/2$ yards
- 1"-wide HeatnBond fusible tape
- Four $3/4$" buttons to cover
- Matching thread for construction
- Rubber bands
- Non-permanent marking pen
- Ruler

Preparation

1 Prewash all washable fabrics and interfacing if you will be laundering this garment.

2 Dampen Fabric 1. Tightly wring the piece of fabric and wrap rubber bands around it as done in tie-dying. Put it in the dryer until dry. Remove rubber bands and smooth fabric to desired texture.

3 Lightly dampen Fabric 2. Using a hot iron and plenty of steam, press irregular "pleats" into fabric by gathering wrinkles in the fabric and ironing as you go. Carefully iron fusible knit interfacing onto the wrong side of this "crinkle-pleated" piece of fabric.

4 Depending on which size vest you are making, you will need to cut approximately 20 three-inch (3") squares from Fabric 1, 35 to 40 three-inch (3") squares from Fabric 2, and 15 to 20 three-inch (3") squares from Fabric 3. Cut two-inch (2") lengths of HeatnBond fusible tape for each square cut.

5 On the straight grain, cut 13 to 15 thirty-inch (30") long strips, $1^1/_4$" wide, from the deep red fabric. See General Instructions: Piecing Bias Strips and Binding on pages 11-12.

6 For the binding, cut, from the deep red fabric, enough two-inch (2") wide bias strips to equal approximately 170 inches for the vest in size medium. You will use a little less bias if you are making the vest in smaller sizes and a little more if you are making the vest in larger sizes. Piece strips together. See General Instructions: Piecing Bias Strips and Binding on pages 11-12.

Construction

1 Set aside two to three squares from each of Fabrics 1, 2, and 3. Fuse the adhesive side of the two-inch (2") HeatnBond fusible tape pieces to the center of the wrong side of the remaining squares. Let all fabrics cool and remove the paper backing.

2 Cut the vest front underlinings from the muslin. On each underlining, make a straight vertical line which is parallel to the center front line using a pencil and ruler. Begin drawing this line at the center of the shoulder seam and continue down to the lower edge.

3 Working on an ironing board, begin positioning the three-inch (3") squares, right sides up, in a row down the vertical line. Alternate squares using Fabrics 2 and 3. In the vertical row next to this, make another row, alternating Fabrics 1 and 2. To create this "variation on a checkerboard" pattern, be sure that the Fabric 2 squares are always corner to corner. Fuse each row in place as soon as it is correctly positioned. When you get to the outer edges of the vest front underlinings, you will have remaining areas to cover which are too small for full $^3/_4$" squares. Cut and piece from the squares you set aside in Step 1, fusing in place with smaller pieces of the HeatnBond fusible tape.

4 Using the straight thirty-inch (30") strips, press the long raw edges to the center, making the finished width $^1/_2$". Starting with the horizontal lines, center the binding over the raw edges of the three-inch (3") squares and top-stitch along both sides.

5 Cover raw edges vertically in the same manner as you did in Step 4.

6 RST, stitch the shoulder and side seams of the vest fronts and back. Press seams open.

7 Sew the lining together in the same manner as you did in Step 6.

8 At this time, try on the vest and make any necessary fitting adjustments to both vest and lining.

9 WST, baste the lining to the vest around all raw edges using $1/4$" seam allowance.

10 Bind around vest and arm holes. See General Instructions: Piecing Bias Strips and Binding on pages 11-12.

11 Make horizontal $3/4$" buttonholes on right vest front. If necessary, see General Instructions: Buttons and Buttonholes on page 9.

12 Cover all four $3/4$" buttons with coordinating fabrics and sew buttons onto left vest front.

Crazy
About
Quilting

Crazy About Quilting

Use "Vest B" patterns — see pages 124-125.
All fabrics are 100% cotton.

Materials

	XS	S	M	L	XL
Lining — 45" wide	$7/8$ yd.	1 yd.	$1^1/_4$ yds.	$1^1/_4$ yds.	$1^1/_3$ yds.
Cotton Flannel Underlining — 60" wide	1 yd.	1 yd.	1 yd.	1 yd.	1 yd.
13 Assorted Fabrics for Piecing — 45" wide	8"	8"	8"	8"	8"

For all sizes:
- Binding: $1/2$ yard of fabric
- Four $3/4$" buttons for closure
- Assorted buttons for decoration
- Matching thread for construction
- Coordinating thread for machine embroidery stitching
- Invisible thread for top-stitching
- #3 pearl cotton for hand embroidery (optional)
- #18 tapestry needle (optional)
- Non-permanent marking pen

Preparation

1 Cut two (2) pieces of cotton flannel underlining for the vest fronts and allow at least two inches (2") around all sides of the pattern piece for shrinkage after quilting. Do not cut the pattern shape yet.

2 From the 13 assorted fabrics chosen for piecing, cut $3^1/_2$" strips.

3 From the lining fabric, cut the vest fronts and back.

4 For the binding, cut enough two-inch (2") wide bias strips to equal approximately 170 inches for the vest in size medium. You will use a little less bias if you are making the vest in smaller sizes and a little more if you are making the vest in larger sizes. Piece strips together. See General Instructions: Piecing Bias Strips and Binding on pages 11-12.

Crazy-Quilting

1 From a dark solid fabric, cut a piece with five (5) sides measuring $3^1/_2$" at the widest point. Pin the center piece onto the cotton flannel underlining for the vest fronts. For best results, position the first piece of fabric in different places on both vest front pieces.

2 RST and matching raw edges, stitch one raw edge of the second piece of fabric to the raw edge of the five-sided center piece using $1/_4$" seam allowance. To reduce bulk, trim the seam allowance to $1/_8$". Press the seam.

Note: You must press each piece before adding the next.

3 RST and matching raw edges, cover both the center piece and the piece that you just added with a third fabric. Stitch in place using $1/4$" seam allowance and trim off the excess. To reduce bulk, trim the seam allowance to $1/8$". Press the seam.

4 Continue adding different fabrics around the center piece, remembering to cover the piece previously added. Trim seams and press.

5 When you have gone completely around the center piece, trim fabrics to create new angles and then continue to add pieces randomly.

6 Continue adding pieces until you have crazy-quilted the entire cotton flannel underlinings for both vest fronts.

7 When you have completed the crazy-quilting, choose four (4) or five (5) decorative machine stitches and a contrasting thread to stitch over each pieced seam. You can also do this by hand with pearl cotton. See General Instructions: Embroidery Stitches on page 20.

8 After completing the embroidery stitching, wash and dry both vest front pieces, vest back, lining, and cotton flannel underlining.

9 Cut out vest back, lining, and cotton flannel underlining.

Construction

1   Baste vest back to cotton flannel underlining.

2   RST, stitch the shoulder and side seams of the vest fronts and back. Press seams open.

3   Sew the lining together in the same manner as you did in Step 2.

4   At this time, try on the vest and make any necessary fitting adjustments to both vest and lining.

5   WST, baste the lining to the vest around all raw edges using $1/4$" seam allowance.

6   Bind around vest and arm holes. See General Instructions: Piecing Bias Strips and Binding on pages 11-12.

7   Make horizontal $3/4$" buttonholes on right vest front. If necessary, see General Instructions: Buttons and Buttonholes on page 9.

8   Cover all four $3/4$" buttons with coordinating fabrics and sew buttons onto left vest front.

9   Use an assortment of buttons to embellish the vest fronts.

O Christmas Tree!

O Christmas Tree!

Use "Vest A" patterns — see pages 122-123.
All fabrics are 100% cotton.

Materials

	S	M	L	XL	XXL
Texas Cotton — 58" wide	1 yd.	1 yd.	1 yd.	$1^1/_3$ yds.	$1^1/_2$ yds.
Lining — 45" wide	1 yd.	1 yd.	1 yd.	$1^1/_3$ yds.	$1^1/_2$ yds.
Canvas Underlining — 60" wide	$^3/_4$ yd.	$^3/_4$ yd.	$^3/_4$ yd.	$^3/_4$ yd.	$^3/_4$ yd.
Fusible Knit Interfacing — 20" wide	$2^2/_3$ yds.	$2^3/_4$ yds.	$2^3/_4$ yds.	$2^7/_8$ yds.	3 yds.

For all sizes:

- Fabrics: 8" x 8" piece of gold for stars
            5" x 8" piece of green print for tree
            6" x 6" piece of red for hearts
            2" x 2" piece of brown for trunk
- Binding: $^1/_2$ yard of fabric
- HeatnBond Lite iron-on adhesive: $^1/_2$ yard
- Three $^3/_4$" buttons to cover
- Matching thread for construction
- Sulky 40 rayon thread in coordinating colors for appliqués
- Tracing paper for appliqués
- Fine-point black marker
- Non-permanent marking pen

Preparation

1 Prewash all washable fabrics and interfacing if you will be laundering this garment.
Note: If using Texas Cotton, wash and dry twice.

2 Trace all patterns for all appliqués onto tracing paper with a fine-point black marker including broken lines for positioning and/or stitching. Flip tracing paper and place HeatnBond, paper side up, on top of tracing paper pattern. With a pencil, trace the pattern outlines onto the HeatnBond paper backing leaving at least one-inch (1") around all patterns to be traced. Then, cut out the pattern shapes leaving approximately one-half inch ($^1/_2$") around all outlines. Next, place the HeatnBond patterns, paper side up, onto the wrong sides of the fabrics from which they will be cut. Fuse following manufacturer's instructions. Cut these appliqués out along the traced pencil outlines. Do not remove paper backing yet.
Note: Because of the size of some of these appliqué pieces, they are easily misplaced. Set these pieces aside until needed.

3 Cut the vest fronts and back from Texas Cotton, lining, canvas underlining, and fusible knit interfacing.

4 For the binding, cut enough two-inch (2") wide bias strips to equal approximately 158 inches for the vest in size medium. You will use a little less bias if you are making the vest in smaller sizes and a little more if you are making the vest in larger sizes. Piece strips together. See General Instructions: Piecing Bias Strips and Binding on pages 11-12.

This 100% cotton warp knit was originally designed for cotton bale bagging. It is 58-inches wide and loosely knit. When washed, it shrinks at least 25-30% and looks quite different. It also becomes softer and more dense. When using Texas Cotton you should wash the cotton in hot water with detergent and dry on the hottest setting. Then wash and dry again. To stabilize and add body to the fabric, it is best to fuse a layer of lightweight interfacing to the wrong side before constructing a garment. Texas Cotton also dyes beautifully!

Construction

1   WST, fuse the fusible knit interfacing to the vest fronts and back.

2   Remove the paper backing from the large heart, large star, tree, and tree trunk. Place them, adhesive side down, on the left vest front, referring to the photo for placement. Layer as necessary. Fuse following manufacturer's instructions. Let all fabrics cool.

3   Remove the paper backing from the remaining hearts and stars. Referring to the photo for placement, position these appliqué shapes onto the right vest front. Fuse in place. Let all fabrics cool.

4   WST, pin corresponding canvas underlining pieces to vest pieces. In Step 5, you will appliqué onto the vest and canvas underlining as one.

5   Using a satin stitch with coordinating thread, appliqué around the edges of the tree trunk first, then the tree, the heart, and the star. Continue with satin stitch in coordinating thread colors around the remaining appliqué shapes. See General Instructions: Satin Stitching by Machine on pages 12-13.

6   RST, stitch the shoulder and side seams of the vest fronts and back. Press seams open.

7   Sew the lining together in the same manner as you did in Step 6.

8 At this time, try on the vest and make any necessary fitting adjustments to both vest and lining.

9 WST, baste the lining to the vest around all raw edges using $^1/_4$" seam allowance.

10 Bind around vest and arm holes. See General Instructions: Piecing Bias Strips and Binding on pages 11-12.

11 Make horizontal $^3/_4$" buttonholes on right vest front. If necessary, see General Instructions: Buttons and Buttonholes on page 9.

12 Cover all three $^3/_4$" buttons with coordinating fabrics and sew buttons onto left vest front.

O Christmas Tree! Appliqués

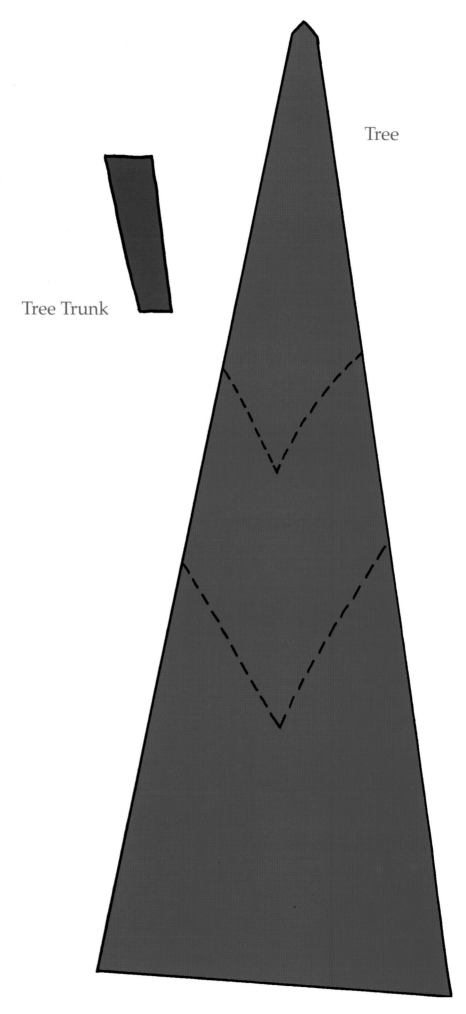

Tree

Tree Trunk

Stars and
Hearts for
Right
Vest Front

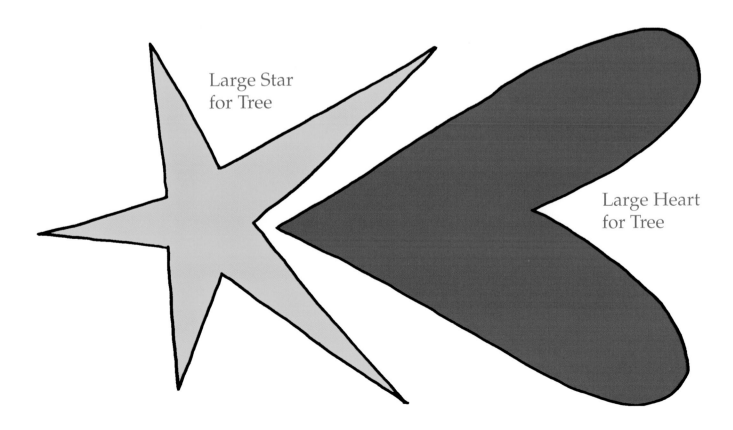

Large Star
for Tree

Large Heart
for Tree

Folk
Heart
Frosty

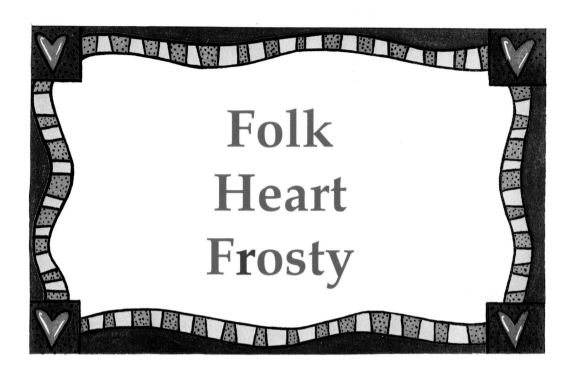

Folk Heart Frosty

Use "Vest F" patterns — see pages 133-134.
All fabrics are 100% cotton.

Materials

	S	M	L	XL
Front and Back — 45" wide	$2/3$ yd.	$7/8$ yd.	$7/8$ yd.	$7/8$ yd.
Lining — 45" wide	$2/3$ yd.	$7/8$ yd.	$7/8$ yd.	$7/8$ yd.
Cotton Batting — 90" wide	$2/3$ yd.	$2/3$ yd.	$2/3$ yd.	$2/3$ yd.

For all sizes:

- Fabrics: 9" x 13" piece of white for snowman and snow
  8" x 8" piece of green for trees
  Scraps for scarf, carrot, heart, arms, hat, and tree trunks
- Binding: $1/2$ yard of coordinating fabric
- HeatnBond Lite iron-on adhesive: $1/2$ yard
- Thirty-two $1/2$" buttons for "snow"
- Matching thread for construction
- Invisible thread for top-stitching
- #3 black pearl cotton for French knots
- #310 black DMC embroidery floss
- #18 tapestry needle
- Tracing paper for appliqués
- Fine-point black marker
- Non-permanent marking pen

Preparation

1 Prewash all washable fabrics if you will be laundering this garment.

2 Trace all patterns for all appliqués onto tracing paper with a fine-point black marker including broken lines for positioning and/or stitching. Flip tracing paper and place HeatnBond, paper side up, on top of tracing paper pattern. With a pencil, trace the pattern outlines onto the HeatnBond paper backing leaving at least one-inch (1") around all patterns to be traced. Then, cut out the pattern shapes leaving approximately one-half inch ($^1/_2$") around all outlines. Next, place the HeatnBond patterns, paper side up, onto the wrong sides of the fabrics from which they will be cut. Fuse following manufacturer's instructions. Cut these appliqués out along the traced pencil outlines. Do not remove paper backing yet.

Note: Because of the size of some of these appliqué pieces, they are easily misplaced. Set these pieces aside until needed.

3 Using a non-permanent marking pen, transfer the markings for placement of the buttons, mouth, eyes, and stitching line for the snow.

4 Cut the vest fronts and back from vest fabric and lining.

5 From the cotton batting, cut two (2) vest fronts and one (1) vest back.

6 For the binding, cut enough two-inch (2") wide bias strips to equal approximately 100 inches for the vest in size medium. You will use a little less bias if you are making the vest in smaller sizes and a little more if you are making the vest in larger sizes. Piece strips together. See General Instructions: Piecing Bias Strips and Binding on pages 11-12.

Construction

1 Remove the paper backing from the following appliqué shapes. Place them, adhesive side down, on the left vest front, referring to the photo for placement. Place them in the following order: snow, snowman, arms, scarf, hat, carrot, and heart. Layer as necessary. Fuse all pieces at once following manufacturer's instructions. Let all fabrics cool.

2 Remove the paper backing from the remaining appliqué shapes. Referring to the photo for placement, position all appliqué shapes onto the right vest front. Place them in the following order: snow, tree trunks, and trees. Fuse in place. Let all fabrics cool.

3 Pin corresponding cotton batting pieces to the wrong sides of vest pieces. In Step 5, you will be stitching the vest and cotton batting as one.

4 Using a very narrow machine satin stitch, appliqué all the shapes with black thread. See General Instructions: Satin Stitching by Machine on pages 12-13.
Note: You do not want the stitch to overpower the design.

5 RST, stitch the shoulder and side seams of the vest fronts and back. Press seams open.

6 Sew the lining together in the same manner as you did in Step 5.

7   At this time, try on the vest and make any necessary fitting adjustments to both vest and lining.

8   WST, baste the lining to the vest around all raw edges using $^{1}/_{4}$" seam allowance.

9   Bind around vest and arm holes. See General Instructions: Piecing Bias Strips and Binding on pages 11-12.

10   Make small French knots for the snowman's eyes, mouth, and buttons. Sew "fringe" on the ends of the scarf using embroidery floss. See General Instructions: Embroidery Stitches on page 10.

11   Referring to the photo for placement, randomly sew on all $^{1}/_{2}$" buttons to look like snow falling on vest fronts.

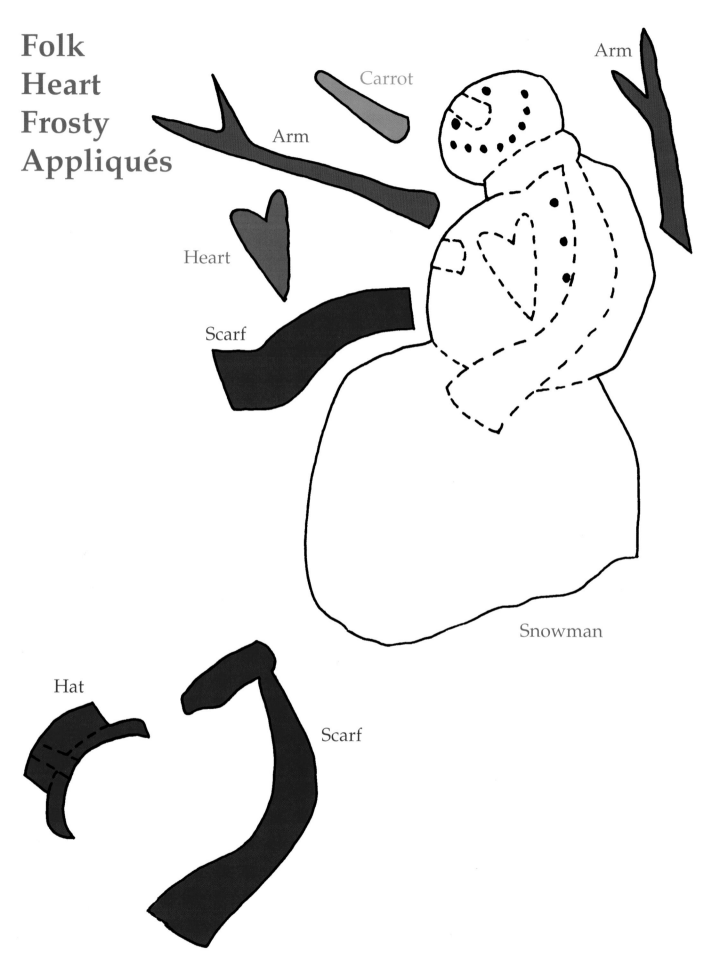

Folk
Heart
Frosty
Appliqués

Carrot

Arm

Arm

Heart

Scarf

Snowman

Hat

Scarf

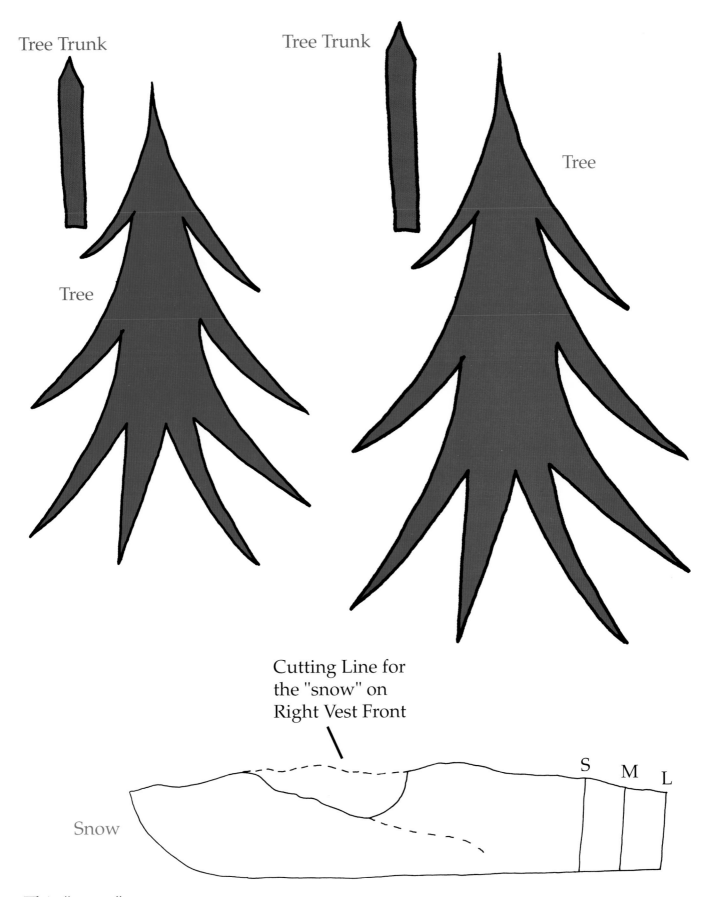

Tree Trunk

Tree Trunk

Tree

Tree

Cutting Line for
the "snow" on
Right Vest Front

S M L

Snow

This "snow" pattern
has been reduced by 50%.
Actual size must be enlarged 200%.

For the Birds

For the Birds

Use "Vest A" patterns — see pages 122-123.
All fabrics are 100% cotton.

Materials

	S	M	L	XL	XXL
Fabric — 45" wide	1 yd.	1 yd.	1 yd.	$1^1/_3$ yds.	$1^1/_2$ yds.
Lining — 45" wide	1 yd.	1 yd.	1 yd.	$1^1/_3$ yds.	$1^1/_2$ yds.
Cotton Batting — 90" wide	$^7/_8$ yd.	$^7/_8$ yd.	$^7/_8$ yd.	$1^1/_8$ yds.	$1^1/_8$ yds.

For all sizes:

- Fabrics: $^1/_8$ yard of gold for birds and binding
  $^1/_8$ yard of red for birdhouse #1, chimney, and binding
  $^1/_8$ yard of blue for birdhouse #2 and binding
  $^1/_4$ yard of green for birdhouses #3 and #5 and binding
  $^1/_4$ yard of orange for birdhouse #4 and binding
  5" x 13" piece of black for birdhouse poles and holes
  Scraps of coordinating fabrics for "laundry," roofs, and birdhouse bases
- HeatnBond Lite iron-on adhesive: $^1/_2$ yard
- Three $^3/_4$" buttons to cover
- Matching thread for construction
- Invisible thread for top-stitching
- Sulky 40 rayon thread in coordinating colors for appliqués
- Tracing paper for appliqués
- Fine-point black marker
- Non-permanent marking pen
- Permanent black fabric marker

Preparation

1   Prewash all washable fabrics if you will be laundering this garment.

2   Trace all patterns for all appliqués onto tracing paper with a fine-point black marker including broken lines for positioning and/or stitching. Flip tracing paper and place HeatnBond, paper side up, on top of tracing paper pattern. With a pencil, trace the pattern outlines onto the HeatnBond paper backing leaving at least one-inch (1") around all patterns to be traced. Then, cut out the pattern shapes leaving approximately one-half inch ($^1/_2$") around all outlines. Next, place the HeatnBond patterns, paper side up, onto the wrong sides of the fabrics from which they will be cut. Fuse following manufacturer's instructions. Cut these appliqués out along the traced pencil outlines. Do not remove paper backing yet.

Note: Because of the size of some of these appliqué pieces, they are easily misplaced. Set these pieces aside until needed. Birdhouse poles will be cut later.

3   Cut the vest fronts and back from vest fabric and lining.

4   From the cotton batting, cut two (2) vest fronts and one (1) vest back.

5   Using a permanent black fabric marker, transfer the markings for placement of the wings, eyes, and beaks to both birds.

6   For the binding, cut enough 6" lengths of bias strips from the gold, red, and blue fabrics and enough 8" lengths of bias strips from the green and orange fabrics, two-inches (2") wide, to equal approximately 158 inches when pieced end-to-end for the vest in size medium. You will use a little less bias if you are making the vest in smaller sizes and a little more if you are making the vest in larger sizes. Piece strips together alternating all five colors. See General Instructions: Piecing Bias Strips and Binding on pages 11-12.

Construction

 1. Remove the paper backing from the following appliqué shapes. Place them, adhesive side down, on the right vest front, referring to the photo for placement. Place them in the following order: birdhouses #1 and #3, all coordinating roofs, doors, bases, holes, "laundry" pieces, and bird #1. Layer as necessary. Fuse all pieces at once following manufacturer's instructions. Let all fabrics cool.

 2. Remove the paper backing from the remaining appliqué shapes. Referring to the photo for placement, position all appliqué shapes onto the left vest front. Place them in the following order: birdhouses #2, #4, and #5, all coordinating roofs, doors, bases, holes, and bird #2. Fuse in place. Let all fabrics cool.

 3. Cut a 3" x 13" piece from the black fabric. Apply fusing adhesive to the wrong side. Do not remove paper backing yet. Measure down from each birdhouse base to the lower edge of the vest and cut the poles from the fusible black fabric in corresponding lengths. Each pole can be a different width from $1/4$" to $1/2$". Place each pole under the corresponding house and fuse in place. Let all fabrics cool.

 4. Using a permanent black fabric marker, draw the clothesline between two of the houses, referring to the photo for placement. Draw the birds' legs and the television antennae on the houses.

 5. Pin corresponding cotton batting pieces to the wrong sides of vest pieces. In Step 7 you will be stitching the vest and cotton batting as one.

6. Using a very narrow machine satin stitch, stitch the clothesline and antennae with black thread. Continuing with the black thread, appliqué the poles, birds, and "laundry" pieces. Next, appliqué the birdhouses, doors, roofs, and bases with gold thread. See General Instructions: Satin Stitching by Machine on pages 12-13.

7 RST, stitch the shoulder and side seams of the vest fronts and back. Press seams open.

8 Sew the lining together in the same manner as you did in Step 7.

9 At this time, try on the vest and make any necessary fitting adjustments to both vest and lining.

10 WST, baste the lining to the vest around all raw edges using $1/4$" seam allowance.

11 Bind around vest and arm holes. See General Instructions: Piecing Bias Strips and Binding on pages 11-12.

12 Make horizontal $3/4$" buttonholes on right vest front. If necessary, see General Instructions: Buttons and Buttonholes on page 9.

13 Cover all three $3/4$" buttons with coordinating fabrics and sew buttons onto left vest front.

For the
Birds Appliqués

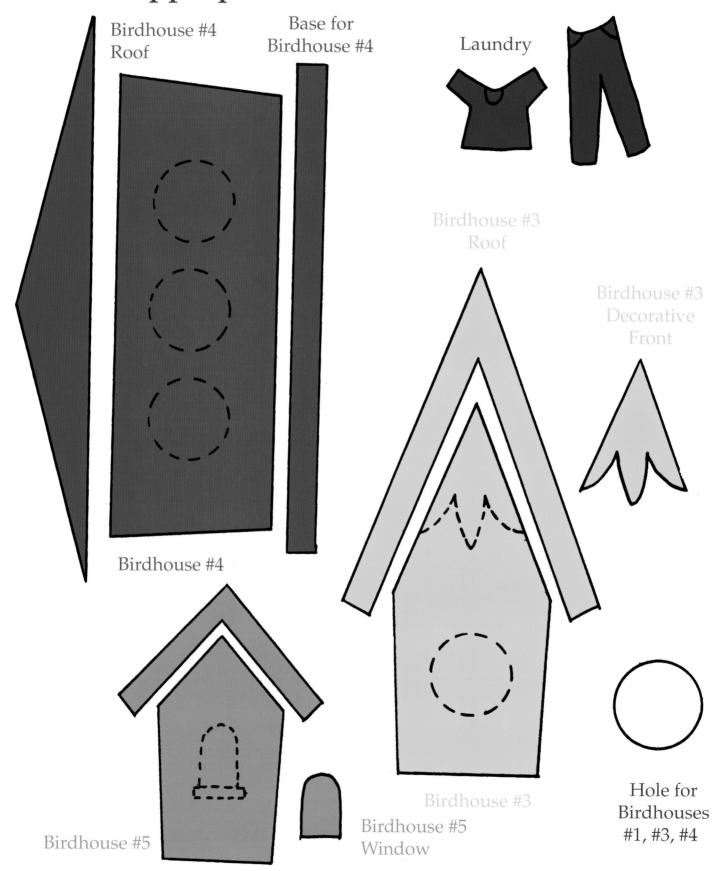

Birdhouse #4
Roof

Base for
Birdhouse #4

Laundry

Birdhouse #3
Roof

Birdhouse #3
Decorative
Front

Birdhouse #4

Birdhouse #5

Birdhouse #3

Birdhouse #5
Window

Hole for
Birdhouses
#1, #3, #4

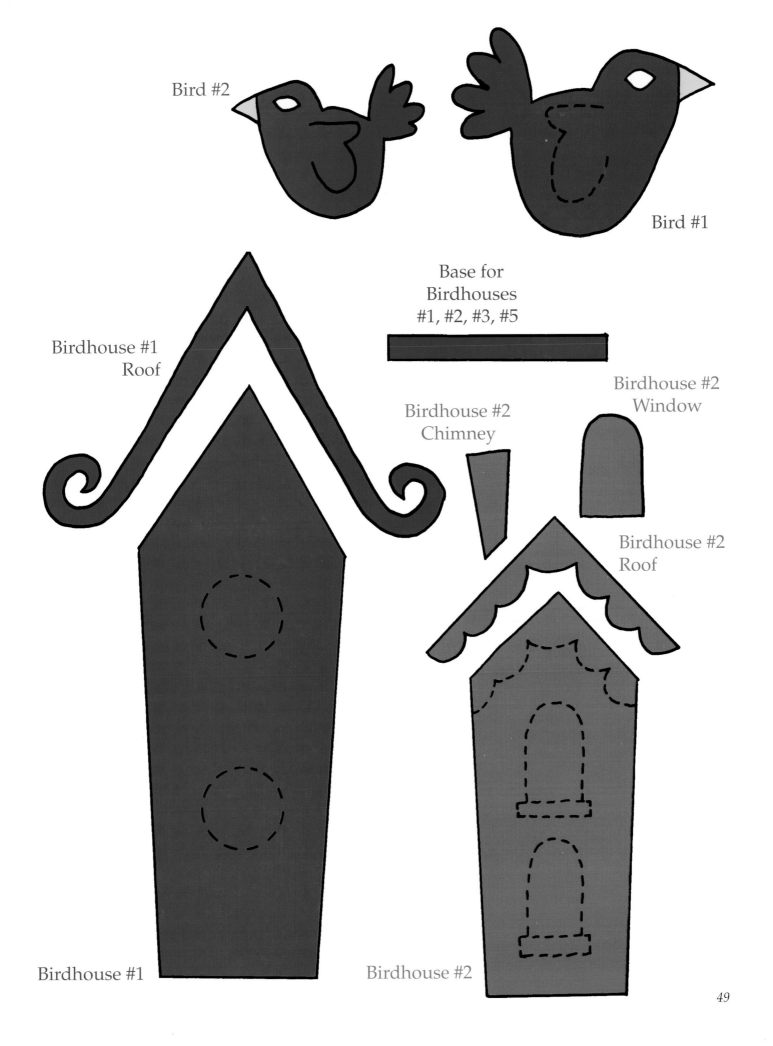

Bird #2

Bird #1

Birdhouse #1
Roof

Base for
Birdhouses
#1, #2, #3, #5

Birdhouse #2
Window

Birdhouse #2
Chimney

Birdhouse #2
Roof

Birdhouse #1

Birdhouse #2

49

Here Comes the Sun!

Here Comes the Sun!

Use "Vest A" patterns — see pages 122-123.
All fabrics are 100% cotton.

Materials

	S	M	L	XL	XXL
Fabric 1: Blue — 45" wide	1 yd.	1 yd.	1 yd.	$1^1/_4$ yds.	2 yds.
Fabric 2: Gold — 45" wide	1 yd.	1 yd.	1 yd.	1 yd.	2 yds.
Cotton Batting — 90" wide	$^7/_8$ yd.	$^7/_8$ yd.	$^7/_8$ yd.	$1^1/_8$ yds.	$1^1/_8$ yds.

For all sizes:

- Fabrics: 4" x 4" piece of orange for cheeks
    4" x 4" piece of white for eyes
- HeatnBond Lite iron-on adhesive: $^1/_2$ yard
- Three $^3/_4$" buttons to cover
- Matching thread for construction
- Invisible thread for top-stitching and quilting
- Sulky 40 rayon thread in coordinating colors for appliqués
- Safety pins
- Tracing paper for appliqués
- Fine-point black marker
- Non-permanent marking pen

Preparation

 1 Prewash all washable fabrics if you will be laundering this garment.

 2 Trace all patterns for all appliqués onto tracing paper with a fine-point black marker including broken lines for positioning and/or stitching. Flip tracing paper and place HeatnBond, paper side up, on top of tracing paper pattern. With a pencil, trace the pattern outlines onto the HeatnBond paper backing leaving at least one-inch (1") around all patterns to be traced. Then, cut out the pattern shapes leaving approximately one-half inch ($^1/_2$") around all outlines. Next, place the HeatnBond patterns, paper side up, onto the wrong sides of the fabrics from which they will be cut. Fuse following manufacturer's instructions. Cut these appliqués out along the traced pencil outlines. Do not remove paper backing yet.

Note: Because of the size of some of these appliqué pieces, they are easily misplaced. Set these pieces aside until needed.

 3 Cut approximately 20 two and one-half inch ($2^1/_2$") squares from Fabrics 1 and 2.

 4 From Fabric 1, cut the right vest front and the vest lining.

5 From Fabric 2, cut the vest back.

6   From the cotton batting, cut two (2) vest fronts and one (1) vest back.

7   For the binding, cut enough two-inch (2") wide bias strips to equal approximately 158 inches for the vest in size medium. You will use a little less bias if you are making the vest in smaller sizes and a little more if you are making the vest in larger sizes. Piece strips together. See General Instructions: Piecing Bias Strips and Binding on pages 11-12.

Construction

1   RST, stitch one side of one Fabric 1 square and one Fabric 2 square together using a $1/4$" seam allowance. Press seam allowance toward the darker fabric. Continue this process until you have a row of squares that is at least as long as the width of the bottom of the vest front. For the vest in size medium, it takes six (6) squares. Continue creating rows that are the same length, alternating colors at the beginning of each row.

2   RST, pin one row on top of another, matching seams and raw edges, to create a checkerboard pattern. Stitch these rows together using a $1/4$" seam along the long edges. Press seams toward bottom row. Continue this process until your left vest front pattern will fit inside the checkerboard fabric you have created. For the vest in size medium, it takes 11 rows from top to bottom.

3 Lining up the center front edge of the vest front pattern with the raw edge of your checkerboard fabric, pin the pattern to the fabric and cut out the left vest front.

*Note: Because there is only one pattern piece for the vest fronts, be sure you place your pattern so that you will be cutting the **left** front.*

4 Pin corresponding cotton batting pieces to the wrong sides of vest pieces. In Step 5 you will be stitching the vest and cotton batting as one.

5 RST, stitch the shoulder and side seams of the vest fronts and back. Press seams open.

6 Sew the lining together in the same manner as you did in Step 5.

7 At this time, try on the vest and make any necessary fitting adjustments to both vest and lining.

8 Remove the paper backing from the blue parts of the eyes, the white parts of the eyes, and the cheeks. Place them, adhesive side down, on the sun's face, referring to the photo or the broken lines on the pattern for placement. Layer as necessary. Fuse following manufacturer's instructions. Let all fabrics cool.

9   Remove the paper backing from the remaining appliqué shapes. Referring to the photo for placement, position all appliqué shapes onto the right vest front. Fuse in place. Let all fabrics cool.

10   WST, baste the lining to the vest around all raw edges using $1/4$" seam allowance. Pin the layers together with safety pins.

11   On the left vest front, using invisible thread, do a quilting stitch, by hand or by machine, along all seam lines of the checkerboard through all layers. If desired, do the same along the side and shoulder seams of the vest.

12   Using a satin stitch with coordinating thread, appliqué around the edges of the sun and stars. Continue the satin stitch in coordinating thread colors around the edges of the sun's face and facial features. See General Instructions: Satin Stitching by Machine on pages 12-13.

13   Bind around vest and arm holes. See General Instructions: Piecing Bias Strips and Binding on pages 11-12.

14   Make horizontal $3/4$" buttonholes on right vest front. If necessary, see General Instructions: Buttons and Buttonholes on page 9.

15   Cover all three $3/4$" buttons with coordinating fabrics and sew buttons onto left vest front.

Here Comes the Sun! Appliqués

Blue of the Eyes

White of the Eyes

Cheeks

The "Stars" patterns used in this vest can be found on page 65.

Sun

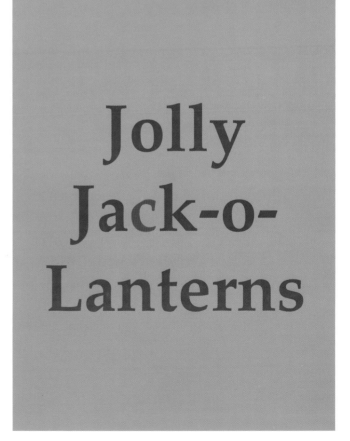

Jolly Jack-o-Lanterns

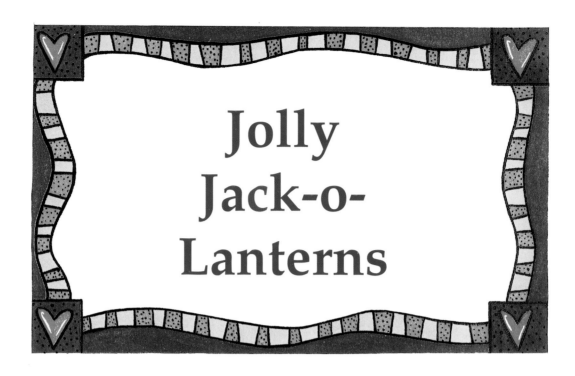

Jolly Jack-o-Lanterns

Use "Vest F" patterns — see pages 133-134.
All fabrics are 100% cotton.

Materials

	S	M	L	XL
Front and Back — 45" wide	$^2/_3$ yd.	$^7/_8$ yd.	$^7/_8$ yd.	$^7/_8$ yd.
Lining — 45" wide	$^2/_3$ yd.	$^7/_8$ yd.	$^7/_8$ yd.	$^7/_8$ yd.
Muslin Underlining — 45" wide	$^2/_3$ yd.	$^2/_3$ yd.	$^2/_3$ yd.	$^2/_3$ yd.

For all sizes:

- Fabrics: 7" x 12" piece of orange for pumpkins
      10" x 10" piece of gold for pumpkin faces and stars
      2" x 2" piece of green for pumpkin stems
      3" x 3" piece of white for moon
- Binding: $^1/_2$ yard of coordinating fabric
- HeatnBond Ultra Hold iron-on adhesive: $1^1/_2$ yards
- Matching thread for construction
- Invisible thread for top-stitching
- Duncan Scribbles Fabric Writer: Gold Platinum SC315
- Tracing paper for appliqués
- Fine-point black marker

Preparation

1 Prewash all washable fabrics if you will be laundering this garment.

2 Trace all patterns for all appliqués onto tracing paper with a fine-point black marker including broken lines for positioning and/or stitching. Flip tracing paper and place HeatnBond, paper side up, on top of tracing paper pattern. With a pencil, trace the pattern outlines onto the HeatnBond paper backing leaving at least one-inch (1") around all patterns to be traced. Then, cut out the pattern shapes leaving approximately one-half inch ($^1/_2$") around all outlines. Next, place the HeatnBond patterns, paper side up, onto the wrong sides of the fabrics from which they will be cut. Fuse following manufacturer's instructions. Cut these appliqués out along the traced pencil outlines. Do not remove paper backing yet.

Note: Because of the size of some of these appliqué pieces, they are easily misplaced. Set these pieces aside until needed.

3 Cut the vest fronts and back from vest fabric and lining. Cut the vest fronts only from the muslin underlining and HeatnBond.

4 For the vest fronts, fuse the HeatnBond onto the muslin underlining following manufacturer's instructions. Cut out pieces. Do not remove paper backing yet.

5 For the binding, cut enough two-inch (2") wide bias strips to equal approximately 100 inches for the vest in size medium. You will use a little less bias if you are making the vest in smaller sizes and a little more if you are making the vest in larger sizes. Piece strips together. See General Instructions: Piecing Bias Strips and Binding on pages 11-12.

Construction

 1   Remove the paper backing from the muslin underlining pieces for the vest fronts. WST, fuse the vest front fabric to the muslin underlining following manufacturer's instructions. Let all fabrics cool.

 2   RST, stitch the shoulder and side seams of the vest fronts and back. Press seams open.

 3   Sew the lining together in the same manner as you did in Step 2.

 4   At this time, try on the vest and make any necessary fitting adjustments to both vest and lining.

5   WST, baste the lining to the vest around all raw edges using $1/4$" seam allowance.

 6   Bind around vest and arm holes. See General Instructions: Piecing Bias Strips and Binding on pages 11-12.

7   Remove the paper backing from the eyes, nose, and mouth for Pumpkins A , B, and C. Place them, adhesive side down, on the corresponding pumpkins. Fuse following manufacturer's instructions. Let all fabrics cool.

8   Remove the paper backing from Pumpkins A and B and their stems. Place them, adhesive side down, on the left vest front, referring to the photo for placement. Fuse following manufacturer's instructions. Let all fabrics cool.

9   Remove the paper backing from Pumpkin C and its stem. Place them, adhesive side down, on the right vest front, referring to the photo for placement. Fuse following manufacturer's instructions. Let all fabrics cool.

10   Remove the paper backing from the stars and randomly position, adhesive side down, on both vest fronts, referring to the photo for placement. Fuse following manufacturer's instructions. Let all fabrics cool.

11   Using the Scribbles Fabric Writer, outline the raw edges of all appliqué pieces. Embellish, as desired, with additional painted lines. Use a steady hand and pressure on the bottle. Any stray paint splatters can easily be removed with a straight pin or toothpick.

12   Dry flat four (4) to six (6) hours. The paint will cure completely in 24 hours and the garment can be washed in 72 hours. To launder, turn inside out and wash in warm water on delicate cycle. Tumble dry on low heat.

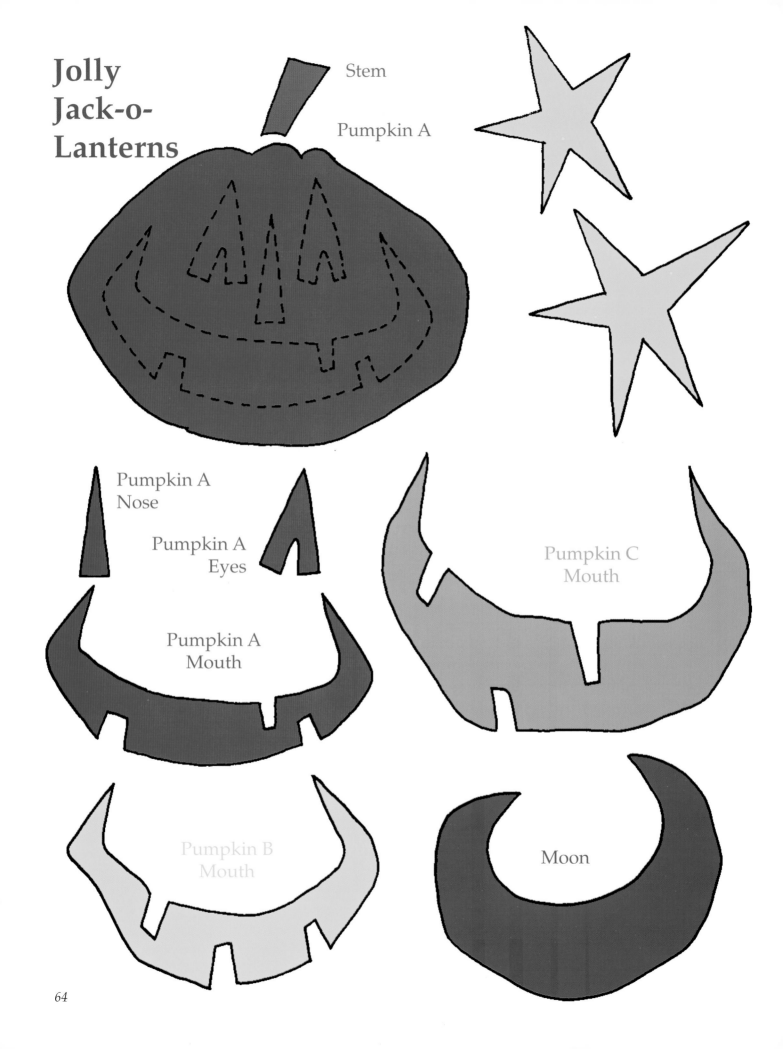

Jolly Jack-o-Lanterns

Stem

Pumpkin A

Pumpkin A
Nose

Pumpkin A
Eyes

Pumpkin A
Mouth

Pumpkin C
Mouth

Pumpkin B
Mouth

Moon

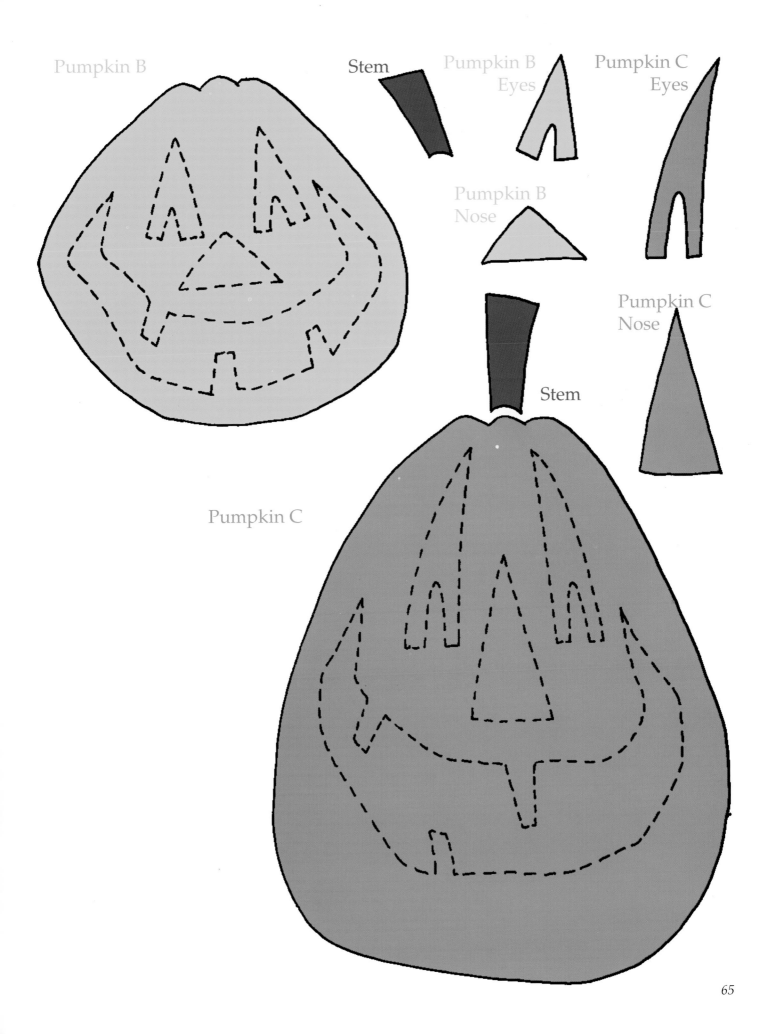

Pumpkin B

Stem

Pumpkin B
Eyes

Pumpkin C
Eyes

Pumpkin B
Nose

Pumpkin C
Nose

Stem

Pumpkin C

Lots
of
Love

Lots of Love

Use "Vest D" patterns — see pages 129-130.
All fabrics are 100% cotton.

Materials

	XS	S	M	L	XL
Right Front Vest Fabric — 45" wide	15" x 18"	15" x 18"	15" x 18"	15" x 18"	15" x 18"
Left Front and Back Vest Fabric — 45" wide	$5/8$ yd.	$5/8$ yd.	$5/8$ yd.	$5/8$ yd.	$5/8$ yd.
Lining and Binding Fabric — 45" wide	1 yd.	1 yd.	1 yd.	1 yd.	$1^{1}/4$ yds.
Cotton Batting — 90" wide	$5/8$ yd.	$5/8$ yd.	$5/8$ yd.	$5/8$ yd.	$5/8$ yd.

For all sizes:
- Fabric: 4" x 7" piece of coordinating fabric for heart
- Matching thread for construction
- Sulky 40 rayon thread in a coordinating color for appliqué
- Straight pins
- Tracing paper for appliqué
- Fine-point black marker
- Non-permanent marking pen

Preparation

1   Prewash all washable fabrics if you will be laundering this garment.

2   Cut the vest fronts and back from vest fabrics and lining.

3   From the cotton batting, cut two (2) vest fronts and one (1) vest back.

4   For the binding, cut enough two-inch (2") wide bias strips to equal approximately 134 inches for the vest in size medium. You will use a little less bias if you are making the vest in smaller sizes and a little more if you are making the vest in larger sizes. Piece strips together. See General Instructions: Piecing Bias Strips and Binding on pages 11-12.

Construction

1 Pin corresponding cotton batting pieces to the wrong sides of vest pieces. In Step 2 you will be stitching the vest and cotton batting as one.

2 RST, stitch the shoulder and side seams of the vest fronts and back. Press seams open.

3 Sew the lining together in the same manner as you did in Step 2.

4 At this time, try on the vest and make any necessary fitting adjustments to both vest and lining.

5 WST, baste the lining to the vest around all raw edges using $1/4$" seam allowance.

Quilting

1 To quilt the right vest front and the appliquéd heart, you will be using what Patrick calls the "vermicelli" stitch. This stitch is done in a free-form manner and resembles vermicelli noodles. To learn this stitch, see General Instructions: Vermicelli Stitch on page 13.

2 After mastering the "vermicelli" stitch, quilt the entire right front of the vest. Because your shoulder and side seams have already been stitched, be careful not to pucker fabric toward these seams as you move from the center outward.

3 Trace the heart pattern onto tracing paper with a fine-point black marker. Cut the heart pattern from the fabric you have chosen. Referring to the photo for placement, place the heart on the left vest front and secure it with straight pins. Starting in the middle of the heart, begin quilting using the "vermicelli" stitch, stitching to the raw edges of the heart.

4 Using a non-permanent marking pen, randomly draw "rays" shooting out from the heart. These lines should begin $^1/_4$" to $^1/_2$" from the edge of the heart and should not be longer than $1^1/_4$".

5 Using a satin stitch with coordinating thread, appliqué around the edges of the heart and stitch over the lines for the "rays" of the heart. See General Instructions: Satin Stitching by Machine on pages 12-13.

6 Bind around vest and arm holes. See General Instructions: Piecing Bias Strips and Binding on pages 11-12.

Lots
of
Love

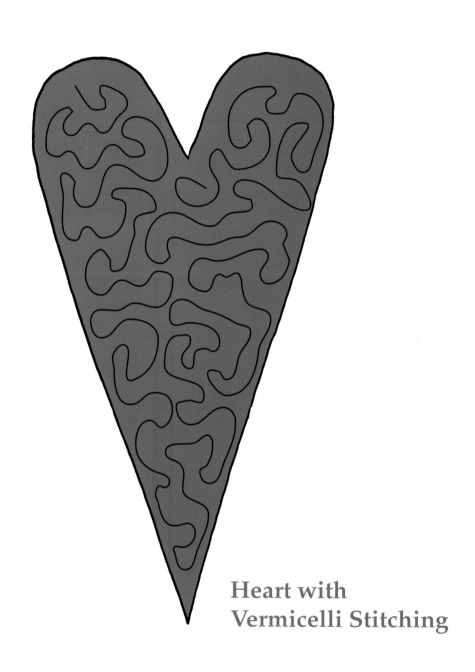

**Heart with
Vermicelli Stitching**

Lots
of
Love
Appliqué

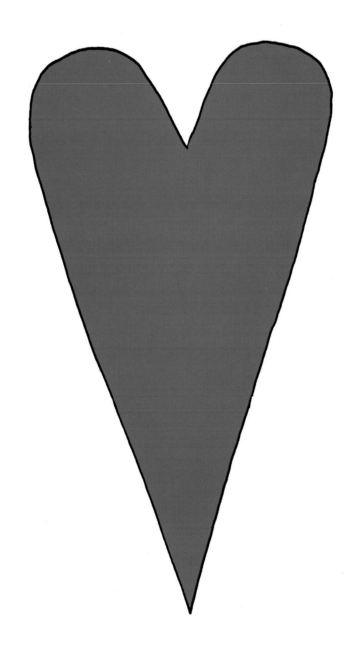

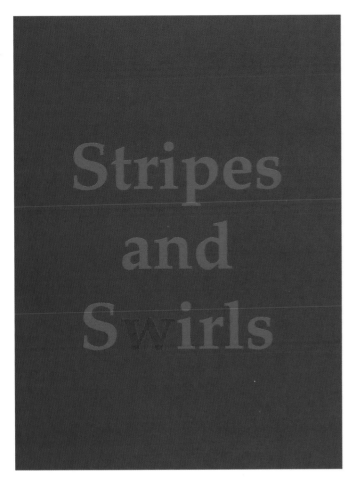

Stripes
and
Swirls

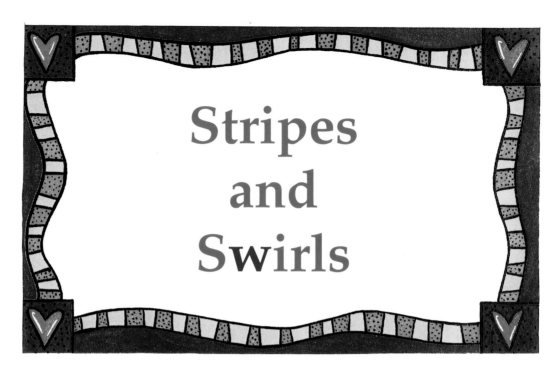

Stripes and Swirls

Use "Vest E" patterns — see pages 131-132.
All fabrics are 100% cotton.

Materials

	S	M	L	XL
Front and Back — 45" wide	$^7/_8$ yd.	$1^1/_8$ yds.	$1^1/_8$ yds.	$1^1/_4$ yds.
Lining — 45" wide	$^7/_8$ yd.	$1^1/_8$ yds.	$1^1/_8$ yds.	$1^1/_4$ yds.
Canvas Underlining — 60" wide	$^7/_8$ yd.	$^7/_8$ yd.	$^7/_8$ yd.	$^7/_8$ yd.
1" Elastic	6"	6"	$6^1/_2$"	7"

For all sizes:

- Fabrics: $^1/_2$ yard of gold for swirls, stripes, and bias
  $^1/_2$ yard of red for swirls, stripes, and bias
- HeatnBond Lite iron-on adhesive: 2 yards
- Matching thread for construction
- Sulky 40 rayon thread in gold for appliqués
- Sulky 40 rayon thread in red for appliqués
- Bodkin or safety pin
- Tracing paper for appliqués
- Fine-point black marker
- Non-permanent marking pen

Preparation

1 Prewash all washable fabrics if you will be laundering this garment.

2 Trace all patterns for all appliqués onto tracing paper with a fine-point black marker including broken lines for positioning and/or stitching. Flip tracing paper and place HeatnBond, paper side up, on top of tracing paper pattern. With a pencil, trace the pattern outlines onto the HeatnBond paper backing leaving at least one-inch (1") around all patterns to be traced. Then, cut out the pattern shapes leaving approximately one-half inch (¹/₂") around all outlines. Next, place the HeatnBond patterns, paper side up, onto the wrong sides of the fabrics from which they will be cut. Fuse following manufacturer's instructions. Cut these appliqués out along the traced pencil outlines. Do not remove paper backing yet.

Note: Because of the size of some of these appliqué pieces, they are easily misplaced. Set these pieces aside until needed.

3 Cut the vest fronts and back from vest fabric, lining, and canvas underlining. Cut vest fronts from the HeatnBond. Cut elastic to the correct length for your vest.

4 For the vest fronts, fuse the HeatnBond to the canvas underlining following manufacturer's instructions. Cut out pieces. Do not remove backing yet.

5 For the binding, cut enough two-inch (2") wide bias strips to equal approximately 110 inches for the vest in size medium. You will use a little less bias if you are making the vest in smaller sizes and a little more if you are making the vest in larger sizes. Piece strips together. See General Instructions: Piecing Bias Strips and Binding on pages 11-12.

Construction

1 Remove the paper backing from the canvas underlining for the vest fronts. Place the vest front fabric, WST, on the canvas underlining and fuse into place following manufacturer's instructions. Let all fabrics cool.

2 Remove the paper backing from the swirl shapes. Place them, adhesive side down, on the right vest front, referring to the photo for placement. Fuse all pieces following manufacturer's instructions. Let all fabrics cool.

3 Using a satin stitch with Sulky 40 gold thread, appliqué around the edges of the gold swirls. Continue the satin stitch with Sulky 40 red thread around the edges of the red swirls. See General Instructions: Satin Stitching by Machine on pages 12-13.

4 Remove the paper backing from the stripes. Referring to the photo for placement, position the stripes, alternating gold and red, onto the left vest front. Make sure they are spaced evenly. Cut off the excess. Fuse in place. Let all fabrics cool.

5 Using a satin stitch with Sulky 40 coordinating thread, appliqué around the edges of the gold and red stripes. See General Instructions: Satin Stitching by Machine on pages 12-13.

6 Using a non-permanent marking pen, mark the elastic stitching line on the lining back. WST, match all the raw edges of the vest and lining backs and stitch along the stitching lines. Using a bodkin or a safety pin, thread the elastic through the opening. Stitch across one end of the elastic and continue pulling the elastic. Remove the bodkin/safety pin and stitch across the other end.

7 RST, stitch the shoulder and side seams of the vest fronts and back. Press seams open.

8 Sew the lining together in the same manner as you did in Step 7.

9 At this time, try on the vest and make any necessary fitting adjustments to both vest and lining.

10 WST, baste the lining to the vest around all raw edges using $^1/_4$" seam allowance.

11 Bind around vest and arm holes. See General Instructions: Piecing Bias Strips and Binding on pages 11-12.

Stripes
and
Swirls
Appliqués

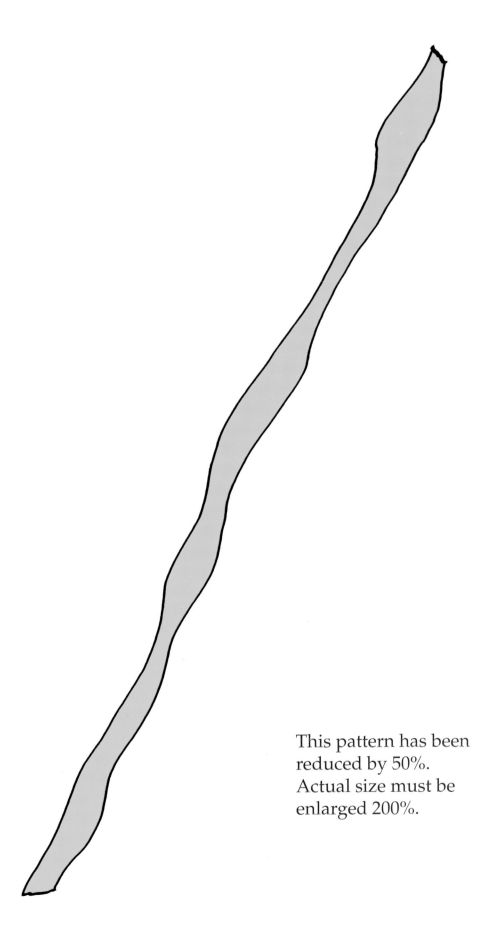

This pattern has been
reduced by 50%.
Actual size must be
enlarged 200%.

Wishing on a Star

Wishing on a Star

Use "Vest F" patterns — see pages 133-134.
All fabrics are 100% cotton.

Materials

	S	M	L	XL
Front and Back — 45" wide	$2/3$ yd.	$7/8$ yd.	$7/8$ yd.	$7/8$ yd.
Texas Cotton — 58" wide	$2/3$ yd.	$2/3$ yd.	$7/8$ yd.	1 yd.
Lining — 45" wide	$2/3$ yd.	$7/8$ yd.	$7/8$ yd.	$7/8$ yd.
Canvas Underlining— 60" wide	$2/3$ yd.	$2/3$ yd.	$2/3$ yd.	$2/3$ yd.
Fusible Knit Interfacing — 20" wide	$2^2/3$ yds.	$2^3/4$ yds.	$2^3/4$ yds.	$2^7/8$ yds.

For all sizes:

- Fabrics: 8" x 8" piece of gold
            8" x 8" piece of red
- Bias binding: 1 yard of contrasting fabric
- HeatnBond Lite iron-on adhesive: $1/2$ yard
- Matching thread for construction
- Matching thread for bias trim
- Sulky 40 rayon thread in a variegated color for appliqués
- Tracing paper for appliqués
- Fine-point black marker

Preparation

1 Prewash all washable fabrics and interfacing if you will be laundering this garment.

Note: If using Texas Cotton, wash and dry twice.

2 Trace all patterns for all appliqués onto tracing paper with a fine-point black marker including broken lines for positioning and/or stitching. Flip tracing paper and place HeatnBond, paper side up, on top of tracing paper pattern. With a pencil, trace the pattern outlines onto the HeatnBond paper backing leaving at least one-inch (1") around all patterns to be traced. Then, cut out the pattern shapes leaving approximately one-half inch ($^1/_2$") around all outlines. Next, place the HeatnBond patterns, paper side up, onto the wrong sides of the fabrics from which they will be cut. Fuse following manufacturer's instructions. Cut these appliqués out along the traced pencil outlines. Do not remove paper backing yet.

Note: Because of the size of some of these appliqué pieces, they are easily misplaced. Set these pieces aside until needed.

3 Cut the vest fronts and back from Texas Cotton, lining, canvas underlining, and fusible knit interfacing.

4 For the decoration on the vest fronts and back, cut enough bias strips, $1^1/_4$" wide, to equal approximately 90 inches. Piece strips together. See General Instructions: Piecing Bias Strips and Binding on pages 11-12.

5 For the binding, cut enough two-inch (2") wide bias strips to equal approximately 100 inches for the vest in size medium. You will use a little less bias if you are making the vest in smaller sizes and a little more if you are making the vest in larger sizes. Piece strips together. See General Instructions: Piecing Bias Strips and Binding on pages 11-12.

Construction

1 WST, fuse the fusible knit interfacing to the backs of the vest fronts and vest back following manufacturer's instructions. Using the vest fronts and back cut from the Texas Cotton, stitch both side seams, RST, and only the right shoulder seam. Press seams open.

2 Using the decorative bias, press the raw edges to the center of the wrong side of the bias so that your finished width is $1/2$". Start at the unsewn shoulder seam and wind your way down the right vest front, around the bottom of the back, up the vest left front and around the back neck edge, ending at the back right shoulder seam. Be sure to match the bias on the shoulder seam. Top-stitch the bias on both folded edges. Press.

3 RST, stitch the left shoulder seam. Press seam open.

4 Remove the paper backing from the star shapes. Place them, adhesive side down, on the vest fronts, referring to the photo for placement. Fuse all piece following manufacturer's instructions. Let all fabrics cool.

5 Using a satin stitch with the variegated thread, appliqué around the edges of the stars. See General Instructions: Satin Stitching by Machine on pages 12-13.

6 RST, stitch the shoulder and side seams of the vest fronts and back. Press seams open.

7 Sew the lining together in the same manner as you did in Step 6.

8 WST, baste the lining to the vest around all raw edges using $1/4$" seam allowance.

9 Bind around vest and arm holes. See General Instructions: Piecing Bias Strips and Binding on pages 11-12.

Wishing
on a
Star
Appliqués

Building on a Theme

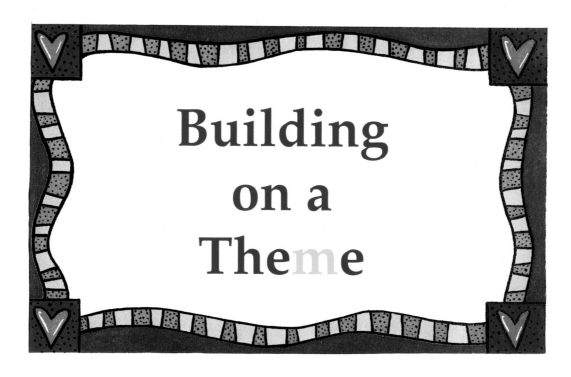

Building on a Theme

Use "Vest C" pattern for Vest Front — see page 126.
Use "Vest B" pattern for Vest Back — see page 125.
All fabrics are 100% cotton.

Materials

	XS	S	M	L	XL
Muslin					
Underlining — 45" wide	$^7/_8$ yd.	1 yd.	$1^1/_4$ yd.	$1^1/_4$ yd.	$1^1/_3$ yd.
Lining — 45" wide	$^7/_8$ yd.	1 yd.	$1^1/_4$ yd.	$1^1/_4$ yd.	$1^1/_3$ yd.

For all sizes:

- Fabrics: 5 quilter's quarters in coordinating prints
- Binding: $^3/_4$ yard of fabric for straight and bias binding
- HeatnBond Lite iron-on adhesive: $1^3/_4$ yard
- Four $^3/_4$" buttons to cover
- Matching thread for construction
- Tracing paper
- Fine-point black marker
- Non-permanent marking pen

Choose several fabric prints with a common theme — music in this case — and mix with other favorite fabrics to create a vest with a "collage" look.

Preparation

1 Prewash all washable fabrics if you will be laundering this garment.

2 Trace the patterns for pieces 1 through 5 from pages 127-128 onto tracing paper with a fine-point black marker.

3 Cut the vest fronts and back from muslin underlining and lining. Cut the vest fronts only from the HeatnBond.

4 Using the fabrics you have chosen, cut out pieces #1 through #5. These pieces do not need to be cut on the straight grain.

Note: We used a different arrangement of fabrics on the left vest front than on the right vest front.

5 For the vest fronts, fuse the HeatnBond onto the muslin underlining following manufacturer's instructions. Cut out pieces. Do not remove paper backing yet.

6 For the decoration on the vest fronts, cut four (4) strips 45" long on the straight grain, $1^1/4$" wide.

7 For the binding, cut enough two-inch (2") wide bias strips to equal approximately 170 inches for the vest in size medium. You will use a little less bias if you are making the vest in smaller sizes and a little more if you are making the vest in larger sizes. Piece strips together. See General Instructions: Piecing Bias Strips and Binding on pages 11-12.

Construction

 1 Remove the paper backing from the muslin underlining pieces for the vest fronts. Arrange pieces #1 through #5 on the muslin fronts as shown on the pattern on page 126. Edges of the sections will butt-up against each other. Fuse following manufacturer's instructions. Let all fabrics cool.

 2 Using the straight 45" strips, press the long raw edges to the center on the wrong side, making the finished width $^1/_2$". Stitch these bindings in order as follows. Begin by positioning a strip over the line where the raw edges of pieces 1 and 2 meet. Top-stitch in place. Stitch a second strip over the line of pieces 2 and 3 and top-stitch. Stitch a strip over the line of 4 and 5 and top-stitch. Finish by covering the last line left to be placed. Repeat for the other vest front piece. Press.

 3 RST, stitch the shoulder and side seams of the vest fronts and back. Press seams open.

 4 Sew the lining together in the same manner as you did in Step 3.

 5 At this time, try on the vest and make any necessary fitting adjustments to both vest and lining.

6 WST, baste the lining to the vest around all raw edges using $^1/_4$" seam allowance.

7 Bind around vest and arm holes. See General Instructions: Piecing Bias Strips and Binding on pages 11-12.

8 Make horizontal $^3/_4$" buttonholes on right vest front. If necessary, see General Instructions: Buttons and Buttonholes on page 9.

9 Cover all four $^3/_4$" buttons with coordinating fabrics and sew buttons onto left vest front.

Birds of a Feather

Use "Jacket A" patterns — see pages 135-138.
All fabrics are 100% cotton.

Materials

	XS	S	M	L	XL
Jacket Fabric — 45" wide	$1^5/8$ yds.	$1^5/8$ yds.	$1^3/4$ yds.	$1^7/8$ yds.	$2^1/8$ yds.
Jacket Fabric — 60" wide	$1^1/2$ yds.	$1^1/2$ yds.	$1^1/2$ yds.	$1^1/2$ yds.	$1^1/2$ yds.
Lining — 45" wide	$1^5/8$ yds.	$1^5/8$ yds.	$1^3/4$ yds.	$1^7/8$ yds.	$2^1/8$ yds.
Lining — 60" wide	$1^1/2$ yds.	$1^1/2$ yds.	$1^1/2$ yds.	$1^1/2$ yds.	$1^1/2$ yds.
Cotton Flannel Underlining — 60" wide	$1^1/2$ yds.	$1^1/2$ yds.	$1^1/2$ yds.	$1^1/2$ yds.	$1^1/2$ yds.

For all sizes:

- Fabrics: $1/4$ yard of green for "vine"
    - 6" x 8" piece of gold for birds
    - 4" x 4" piece of orange for beaks and bellies
    - 8" x 10" piece of green for leaves
- Binding: $1/2$ yard of gold fabric
- HeatnBond Lite iron-on adhesive: $1/2$ yard
- Matching thread for construction
- Invisible thread for top-stitching
- Sulky 40 rayon thread in coordinating colors for appliqués
- About 25 red buttons in two sizes for berries
- Five $3/4$" buttons to cover
- Tracing paper for appliqués
- Fine-point black marker
- Non-permanent marking pen
- Paint for eyes: white acrylic paint mixed with a textile medium
- Permanent black fabric marker
- One pair of 1" shoulder pads

 Prewash all washable fabrics if you will be laundering this garment.

 Trace all patterns for all appliqués onto tracing paper with a fine-point black marker including broken lines for positioning and/or stitching. For the birds, birds' bellies, and beaks, flip the tracing paper pattern before tracing some of the shapes so that some of the birds will face the opposite direction. Flip tracing paper and place HeatnBond, paper side up, on top of tracing paper pattern. With a pencil, trace the pattern outlines onto the HeatnBond paper backing leaving at least one-inch (1") around all patterns to be traced. Then, cut out the pattern shapes leaving approximately one-half inch ($^1/_2$") around all outlines. Next, place the HeatnBond patterns, paper side up, onto the wrong sides of the fabrics from which they will be cut. Fuse following manufacturer's instructions. Cut these appliqués out along the traced pencil outlines. Do not remove paper backing yet.
Note: Because of the size of some of these appliqué pieces, they are easily misplaced. Set these pieces aside until needed. The jacket in the photo on page 94 has 7 birds and 47 leaves.

 Using a non-permanent marking pen, draw the wings and eyes on the birds and the veins on the leaves.

4 Cut the jacket front, back, and sleeves from the jacket fabric, lining, and cotton flannel underlining.

For the vine, cut enough bias strips, $1^1/4$" wide, to wind around the jacket. The total length will depend on how much you curve the vine. See General Instructions: Bias Strips on page 8.

For the binding, cut enough two-inch (2") wide bias strips to equal approximately 134 inches for the jacket in size medium. You will use a little less bias if you are making the jacket in smaller sizes and a little more if you are making the jacket in larger sizes. Piece strips together. See General Instructions: Piecing Bias Strips and Binding on pages 11-12.

Construction

Pin corresponding cotton flannel underlining pieces to the wrong sides of jacket pieces. In Step 2 you will be stitching the jacket and cotton flannel underlining as one.

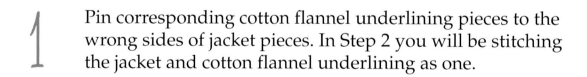

RST, stitch the jacket fronts to the jacket back at the side seams, easing the fronts to match the back between the notches. RST, stitch the shoulder seams. Press seams open.

Sew the lining together in the same manner as you did in Step 2.

At this time, try on the jacket and make any necessary fitting adjustments to both jacket and lining.

Starting at the bottom of the left jacket front, pin the bias "vine" in place, referring to the photo. Wind the vine around the lower back of the jacket, curving the bias tape, and pin into place. Continue to wind the vine up the right jacket front and over the shoulder seam to the upper jacket back, over the left shoulder seam, and end the vine in the upper portion of the left jacket front. Be sure to keep the vine out of the $^3/_8$" seam allowance for jacket binding.

 Using a very narrow machine satin stitch with a coordinating thread, appliqué both sides of the bias trim. See General Instructions: Satin Stitching by Machine on pages 12-13.

 Before removing the paper backing from the birds, remove it from the leaves, beaks, and belly pieces. Place them, adhesive side down, on the birds and fuse following manufacturer's instructions. Let all fabrics cool. Remove the paper backing from the birds. Place the birds and the leaves, adhesive side down, in various places on the vine. Fuse following manufacturer's instructions. Let all fabrics cool.

 Using a very narrow machine satin stitch with a coordinating thread, appliqué the birds and the leaves. See General Instructions: Satin Stitching by Machine on pages 12-13.

 RST, stitch the long, unnotched edges of the sleeve fronts to the same edges of the sleeve backs. Press seams open. To gather the curved top edge of the sleeve between the dots, stitch a row $^1/_2$" and $^3/_4$" from the raw edge with the longest machine stitch. RST, pin sleeve to jacket, matching sleeve seam to shoulder seam. Match notches and raw edges, pulling up gather strings to fit.

10 Sew the lining together in the same manner as you did in Step 9.

WST, baste the lining to the inside of the jacket around all raw edges using $1/4''$ seam allowance.

 Bind the raw edges of the jacket. See General Instructions: Piecing Bias Strips and Binding on pages 11-12.

 Make horizontal $3/4''$ buttonholes on right jacket front. If necessary, see General Instructions: Buttons and Buttonholes on page 9.

 Cover all five $3/4''$ buttons with coordinating fabrics and sew buttons onto left jacket front.

 Using white acrylic paint mixed with a textile medium, paint the eyes on the birds. Outline with a permanent black fabric marker. Draw the upper eye line and color the black pupil. Paint a small white dot inside the pupil. Randomly sew the red buttons onto the jacket for berries. If necessary, refer to the photo for placement.

 Fold the shoulder pads in half to find the center and mark with pins. Turn the jacket inside out and line the pins up with the shoulder seams. Whip-stitch the shoulder pads into place or you may use Velcro or snaps for removable shoulder pads. Try the jacket on to make sure the position of the shoulder pads is correct.

Birds
of a
Feather
Appliqués

Bird

Beak

Belly

Leaves

Fall Finery

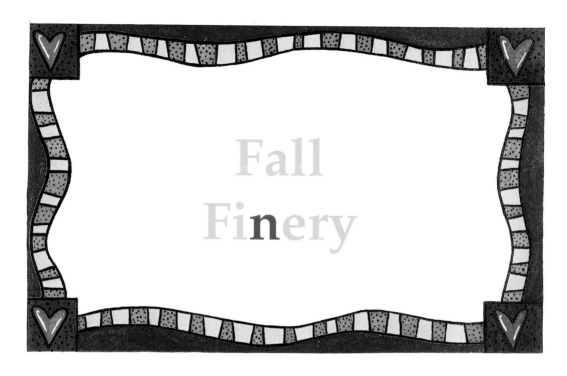

Fall Finery

Use "Jacket A" patterns — see pages 136-139.
All fabrics are 100% cotton.
If using a plaid fabric, allow for matching plaids.

Materials

	XS	S	M	L	XL
Jacket Fabric — 45" wide	$1^5/_8$ yds.	$1^5/_8$ yds.	$1^3/_4$ yds.	$1^7/_8$ yds.	$2^1/_8$ yds.
Jacket Fabric — 60" wide	$1^1/_2$ yds.	$1^1/_2$ yds.	$1^1/_2$ yds.	$1^1/_2$ yds.	$1^1/_2$ yds.
Lining — 45" wide	$1^5/_8$ yds.	$1^5/_8$ yds.	$1^3/_4$ yds.	$1^7/_8$ yds.	$2^1/_8$ yds.
Lining — 60" wide	$1^1/_2$ yds.	$1^1/_2$ yds.	$1^1/_2$ yds.	$1^1/_2$ yds.	$1^1/_2$ yds.
Cotton Flannel Underlining — 60" wide	$1^1/_2$ yds.	$1^1/_2$ yds.	$1^1/_2$ yds.	$1^1/_2$ yds.	$1^1/_2$ yds.

For all sizes:

- Fabrics: Four 10" x 10" pieces in fall colors for leaves
- Binding: $^1/_2$ yard of coordinating fabric
- HeatnBond Lite iron-on adhesive: $^1/_2$ yard
- Matching thread for construction
- Invisible thread for top-stitching
- Sulky 40 rayon thread in coordinating colors for appliqués
- Five $^3/_4$" buttons to cover
- Tracing paper for appliqués
- Fine-point black marker
- Non-permanent marking pen
- One pair of 1" shoulder pads

Preparation

 Prewash all washable fabrics if you will be laundering this garment.

 Trace all patterns for all appliqués onto tracing paper with a fine-point black marker including broken lines for positioning and/or stitching. For the leaves, flip the tracing paper pattern before tracing some of the shapes so that some of the leaves will face the opposite direction. Flip tracing paper and place HeatnBond, paper side up, on top of tracing paper pattern. With a pencil, trace the pattern outlines onto the HeatnBond paper backing leaving at least one-inch (1") around all patterns to be traced. Then, cut out the pattern shapes leaving approximately one-half inch ($^1/_2$") around all outlines. Next, place the HeatnBond patterns, paper side up, onto the wrong sides of the fabrics from which they will be cut. Fuse following manufacturer's instructions. Cut these appliqués out along the traced pencil outlines. Do not remove paper backing yet.

Note: Because of the size of some of these appliqué pieces, they are easily misplaced. Set these pieces aside until needed. The jacket in the photo on page 102 has 14 leaves.

 Using a non-permanent marking pen, draw the veins on the leaves.

 Cut the jacket front, back, and sleeves from the jacket fabric, lining, and cotton flannel underlining.

For the binding, cut enough two-inch (2") wide bias strips to equal approximately 134 inches for the jacket in size medium. You will use a little less bias if you are making the jacket in smaller sizes and a little more if you are making the jacket in larger sizes. Piece strips together. See General Instructions: Piecing Bias Strips and Binding on pages 11-12.

Construction

1   Pin corresponding cotton flannel underlining pieces to the wrong sides of jacket pieces. In Step 2 you will be stitching the jacket and cotton flannel underlining as one.

2   RST, stitch the jacket fronts to the jacket back at the side seams, easing the fronts to match the back between the notches. RST, stitch the shoulder seams. Press seams open.

3   Sew the lining together in the same manner as you did in Step 2.

4   At this time, try on the jacket and make any necessary fitting adjustments to both jacket and lining.

5   Remove the paper backing from the leaves. Place them, adhesive side down, as if they were "falling" from over the right shoulder, down the top of the right sleeve, and across both front pieces to the lower left jacket front and around the back of the jacket. Fuse following manufacturer's instructions. Let all fabrics cool.

6   Using a very narrow machine satin stitch with a coordinating thread, appliqué the leaves and their veins. See General Instructions: Satin Stitching by Machine on pages 12-13.

7   RST, stitch the long, unnotched edges of the sleeve fronts to the same edges of the sleeve backs. Press seams open. To gather the curved top edge of the sleeve between the dots, stitch a row $1/2$" and $3/4$" from the raw edge with the longest machine stitch. RST, pin sleeve to jacket, matching sleeve seam to shoulder seam. Match notches and raw edges, pulling up gather strings to fit.

Sew the lining together in the same manner as you did in Step 7.

 WST, baste the lining to the inside of the jacket around all raw edges using $1/4$" seam allowance.

 Bind the raw edges of the jacket. See General Instructions: Piecing Bias Strips and Binding on pages 11-12.

 Make horizontal $3/4$" buttonholes on right jacket front. If necessary, see General Instructions: Buttons and Buttonholes on page 9.

 Cover all six $3/4$" buttons with coordinating fabrics and sew buttons onto left jacket front.

 Fold the shoulder pads in half to find the center and mark with pins. Turn the jacket inside out and line the pins up with the shoulder seams. Whip-stitch the shoulder pads into place or you may use Velcro or snaps for removable shoulder pads. Try the jacket on to make sure the position of the shoulder pads is correct.

Whimsical Wrap Appliqués

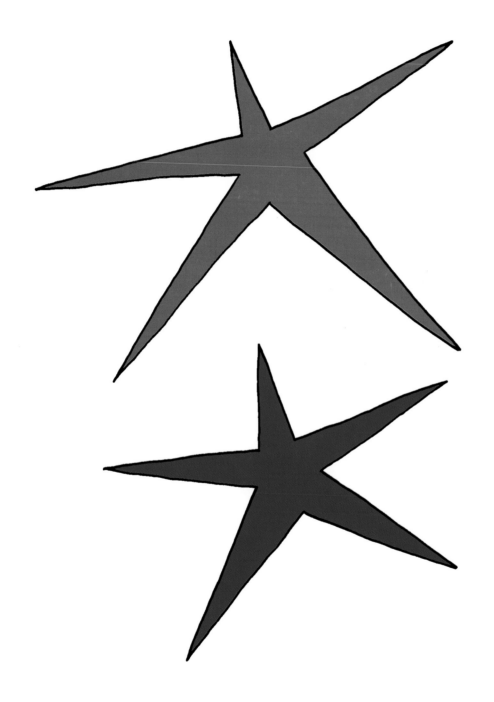

The "Swirls" patterns used in this vest can be found on page 80.

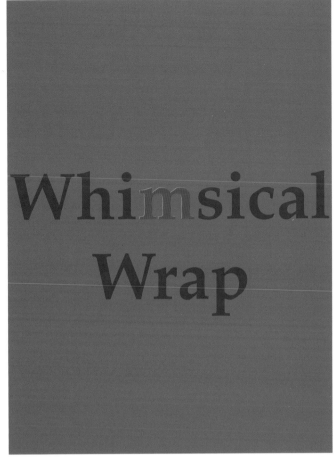

Whimsical Wrap

Whimsical Wrap

Use "Jacket B" patterns — see pages 140-141.
All fabrics are 100% cotton.

Materials

	S	M	L	XL
Front and Back — 45" wide	$3^3/_4$ yds.	4 yds.	4 yds.	4 yds.
Lining — 45" wide	$3^3/_4$ yds.	4 yds.	4 yds.	4 yds.
Cotton Batting — 90" wide	2 yds.	2 yds.	2 yds.	2 yds.

For all sizes:

- Fabrics: $1/_4$ yard of orange for swirls
  $1/_4$ yard of gold for stars
  $1^1/_4$ yards of blue for swirls, cuffs, and binding
- HeatnBond Lite iron-on adhesive: 1 yard
- Matching thread for construction
- Sulky 40 rayon thread in coordinating colors for appliqués
- Six $1^1/_2$" buttons to cover
- Safety pins
- Tracing paper for appliqués
- Fine-point black marker
- Non-permanent marking pen
- One pair of 1" shoulder pads

Preparation

 Prewash all washable fabrics if you will be laundering this garment.

 Trace all patterns for all appliqués onto tracing paper with a fine-point black marker including broken lines for positioning and/or stitching. Flip tracing paper and place HeatnBond, paper side up, on top of tracing paper pattern. With a pencil, trace the pattern outlines onto the HeatnBond paper backing leaving at least one-inch (1") around all patterns to be traced. Then, cut out the pattern shapes leaving approximately one-half inch (¹/₂") around all outlines. Next, place the HeatnBond patterns, paper side up, onto the wrong sides of the fabrics from which they will be cut. Fuse following manufacturer's instructions. Cut these appliqués out along the traced pencil outlines. Do not remove paper backing yet.
Note: Because of the size of some of these appliqué pieces, they are easily misplaced. Set these pieces aside until needed.

 Cut the jacket front, back, and sleeves from the jacket fabric, lining, and cotton batting.

Cut the cuffs from the jacket fabric, making sure to flip the pattern for two of the cuffs.

 For the binding, cut enough two-inch (2") wide bias strips to equal approximately 170 inches for the vest in size medium. You will use a little less bias if you are making the vest in smaller sizes and a little more if you are making the vest in larger sizes. Piece strips together. See General Instructions: Piecing Bias Strips and Binding on pages 11-12.

Construction

1 Pin corresponding cotton batting pieces to the wrong sides of jacket pieces. Secure the cotton batting pieces to the jacket pieces using safety pins. In Step 2 you will be stitching the jacket and cotton batting as one. Position the cuffs onto the ends of the sleeves, securing with safety pins to avoid fabric from moving during the satin stitching. Make sure you have flipped the pattern for two (2) of the cuffs. Satin-stitch the zigzag points of the cuff with matching thread. See General Instructions: Satin Stitching by Machine on pages 12-13.

2 RST, stitch the shoulder/sleeve seams of the jacket front and back. Press seams open.

3 Remove the paper backing from the stars and swirl shapes. Place them, adhesive side down, randomly, referring to the photo for placement. Fuse following manufacturer's instructions. Let all fabrics cool.

4 Using a very narrow machine satin stitch with a coordinating thread, appliqué the stars and swirl shapes.

5 RST, stitch the side/underarm seams of the jacket front and back. Press seams open.

6 Sew the lining together in the same manner as you did in Steps 2 and 5.

7 At this time, try on the jacket and make any necessary fitting adjustments to both jacket and lining.

8 WST, baste the lining to the inside of the jacket around all raw edges using $1/4$" seam allowance.

9 Bind the raw edges of the jacket and cuffs. See General Instructions: Piecing Bias Strips and Binding on pages 11-12.

10 Make horizontal $1^1/2$" buttonholes on right jacket front. If necessary, see General Instructions: Buttons and Buttonholes on page 9.

11 Cover all six $1^1/2$" buttons with three (3) different coordinating fabrics and sew buttons onto left jacket front arranging as desired.

12 Fold the shoulder pads in half to find the center and mark with pins. Turn the jacket inside out and line the pins up with the shoulder seams. Whip-stitch the shoulder pads into place or you may use Velcro or snaps for removable shoulder pads. Try the jacket on to make sure the position of the shoulder pads is correct.

Pic ic
Perfect

Picnic Perfect

Use "Vest G" pattern for Vest Front — see page 135.
Use "Vest F" pattern for Vest Back — see page 133.
Use a purchased skirt pattern.
All fabrics are 100% cotton.

Materials

	S	M	L	XL
Front and Back — 45" wide	$^2/_3$ yd.	$^7/_8$ yd.	$^7/_8$ yd.	$^7/_8$ yd.
"Rind" and Binding — 45" wide	$^2/_3$ yd.	$^2/_3$ yd.	$^3/_4$ yd.	$^3/_4$ yd.
"Melon" — 45" wide	$^2/_3$ yd.	$^2/_3$ yd.	$^3/_4$ yd.	$^3/_4$ yd.
Lining — 45" wide	$^2/_3$ yd.	$^2/_3$ yd.	$^2/_3$ yd.	$^2/_3$ yd.
Canvas Underlining — 60" wide	$^2/_3$ yd.	$^2/_3$ yd.	$^2/_3$ yd.	$^2/_3$ yd.

For all sizes:

- HeatnBond Lite iron-on adhesive: 1 yard
- Matching thread for construction
- Invisible thread for top-stitching
- About 55 brown buttons in assorted sizes for seeds
- Tracing paper
- Fine-point black marker

Preparation

1   Prewash all washable fabrics if you will be laundering these garments.

2   Enlarge the patterns for the rind and the melon on page 135 onto tracing paper with a fine-point black marker. See General Instructions: Enlarging Project Patterns on page 11. Cut out pattern.

3   Cut the vest back from the vest fabric and lining. Cut the vest fronts only from the lining, canvas underlining, and HeatnBond. Cut the "rind" and the "melon" pieces for the vest fronts from the corresponding fabrics.

Note: Be sure to flip your pattern so that you can cut one (1) rind piece and one (1) melon piece for each of the right and the left vest fronts.

4   For the vest fronts, fuse the HeatnBond onto the canvas underlining following manufacturer's instructions. Do not remove paper backing yet.

5   For the binding, cut enough two-inch (2") wide bias strips to equal approximately 100 inches for the vest in size medium. You will use a little less bias if you are making the vest in smaller sizes and a little more if you are making the vest in larger sizes. Piece strips together. See General Instructions: Piecing Bias Strips and Binding on pages 11-12.

Construction

1   Remove the paper backing from the canvas underlining for the vest fronts. WST, fuse the melon fabric onto the adhesive side of the canvas underlining matching all raw edges of the arm holes. Let all fabrics cool.

2   Turn under $1/4$" on inner edge of rind and press. Position the rind overlapping the melon pieces at the inner curve, matching all raw edges.

3   Top-stitch along the inner folded curve of the melon pieces as close as possible to the folded edge.

4   RST, stitch the shoulder and side seams of the vest fronts and back. Press seams open.

5   Sew the lining together in the same manner as you did in Step 4.

6   At this time, try on the vest and make any necessary fitting adjustments to both vest and lining.

7   WST, baste the lining to the vest around all raw edges using $1/4$" seam allowance.

8   Bind around vest and arm holes. See General Instructions: Piecing Bias Strips and Binding on pages 11-12.

Stitch assorted sizes and shades of brown button "seeds" on the melon pieces.

 Using the purchased skirt pattern of your choice, measure and mark five inches (5") above the hemline all the way around the bottom of the pattern to create the border pattern. If the skirt has a front and back pattern, make sure you mark the hemline on both pattern pieces. Do not include hem allowance in this five-inch (5") border. (For example: If the pattern calls for a two-inch (2") hem, measure and mark seven inches (7") above the cutting line for the bottom of the skirt.) Cut your pattern on this line, creating a skirt piece and a hem border piece.

Note: When cutting these pieces from the skirt fabric, be sure to add ⁵/₈" seam allowance to the bottom of the skirt pattern and ⁵/₈" seam allowance to the top of the newly created border pattern.

 RST, stitch the upper edge of the border to the lower edge of the skirt using a ⁵/₈" seam allowance. Trim seams to about ³/₈" and press toward the hem.

 On the border, top-stitch as close to the seam as possible.

 Complete the skirt following the purchased pattern instructions.

 When your skirt is completely finished, stitch assorted sizes and shades of brown button "seeds" around the melon portions of the skirt.

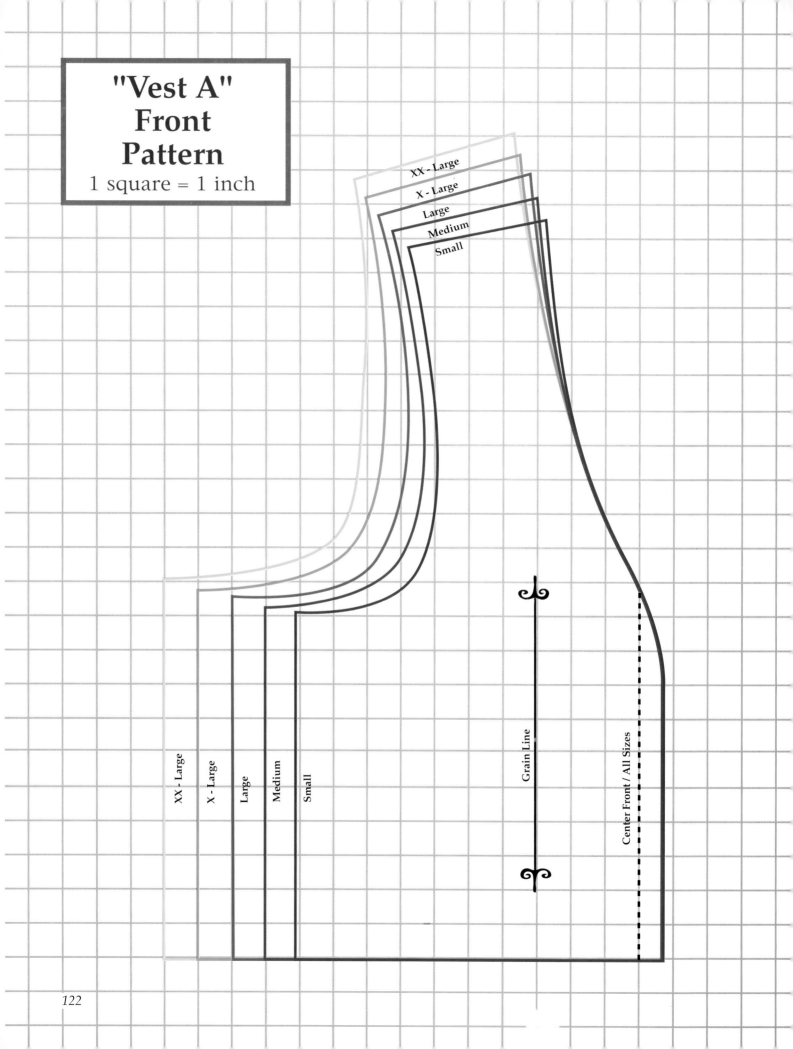

"Vest A"
Front
Pattern
1 square = 1 inch

XX - Large

X - Large

Large

Medium

Small

XX - Large

X - Large

Large

Medium

Small

Grain Line

Center Front / All Sizes

122

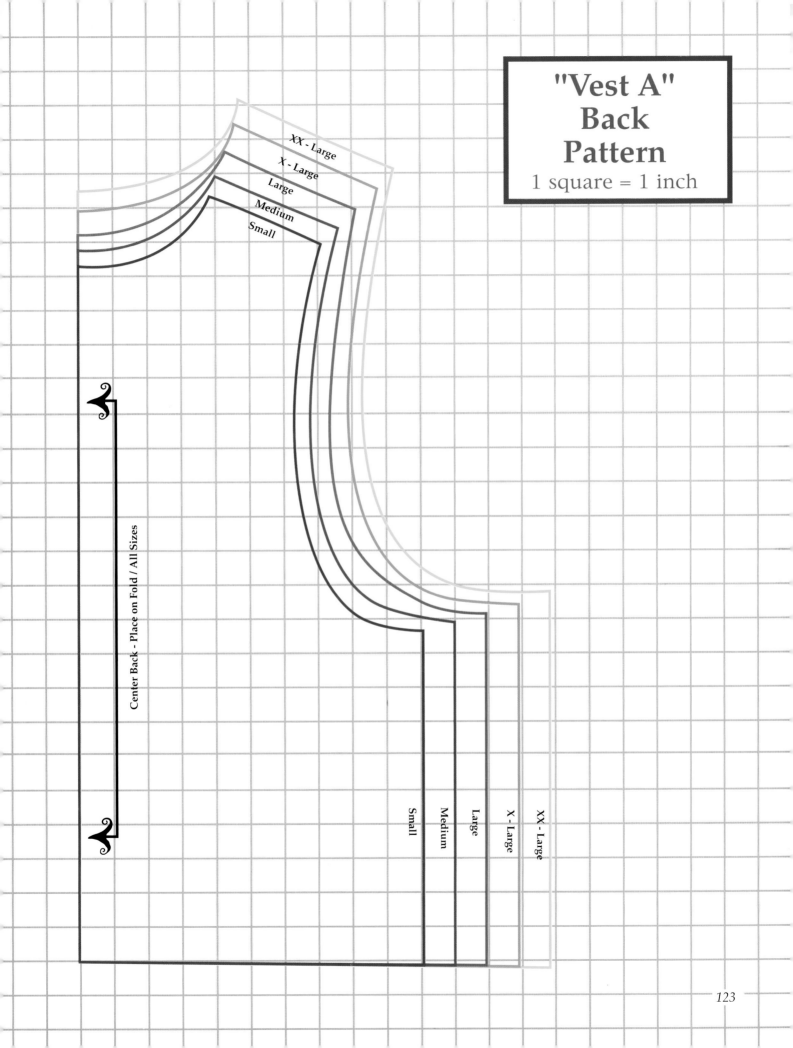

**"Vest A"
Back
Pattern**
1 square = 1 inch

XX - Large

X - Large

Large

Medium

Small

Center Back - Place on Fold / All Sizes

Small

Medium

Large

X - Large

XX - Large

123

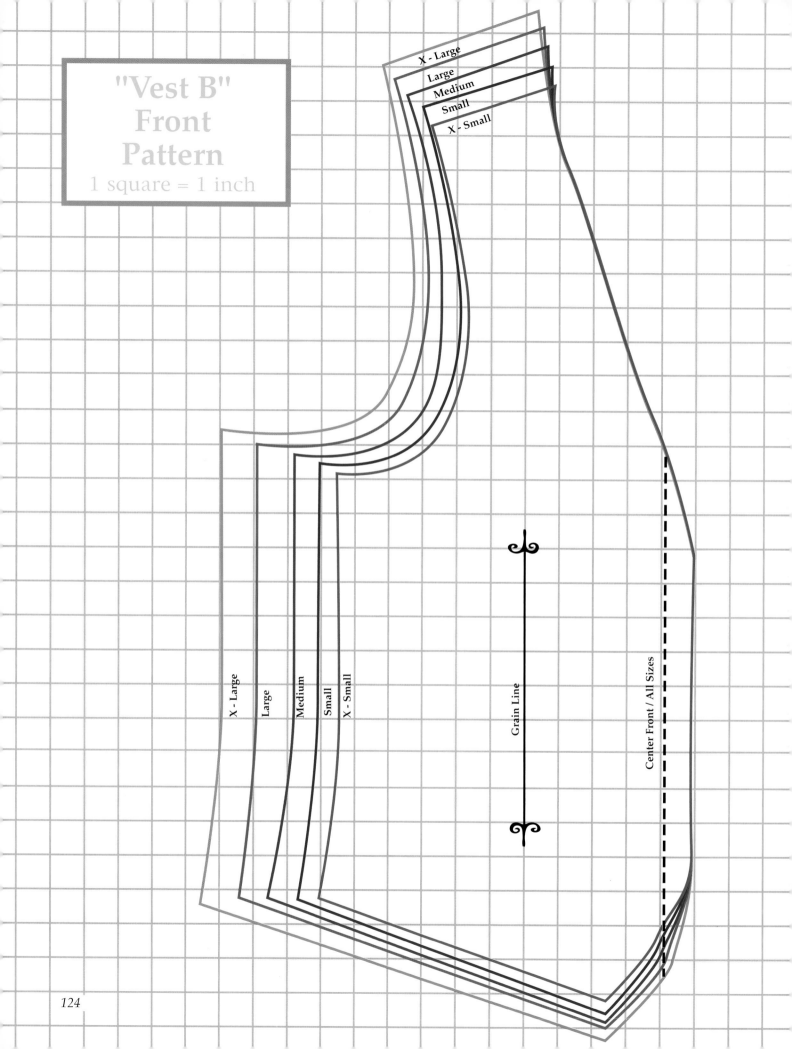

"Vest B"
Front
Pattern
1 square = 1 inch

X - Large
Large
Medium
Small
X - Small

X - Large
Large
Medium
Small
X - Small

Grain Line

Center Front / All Sizes

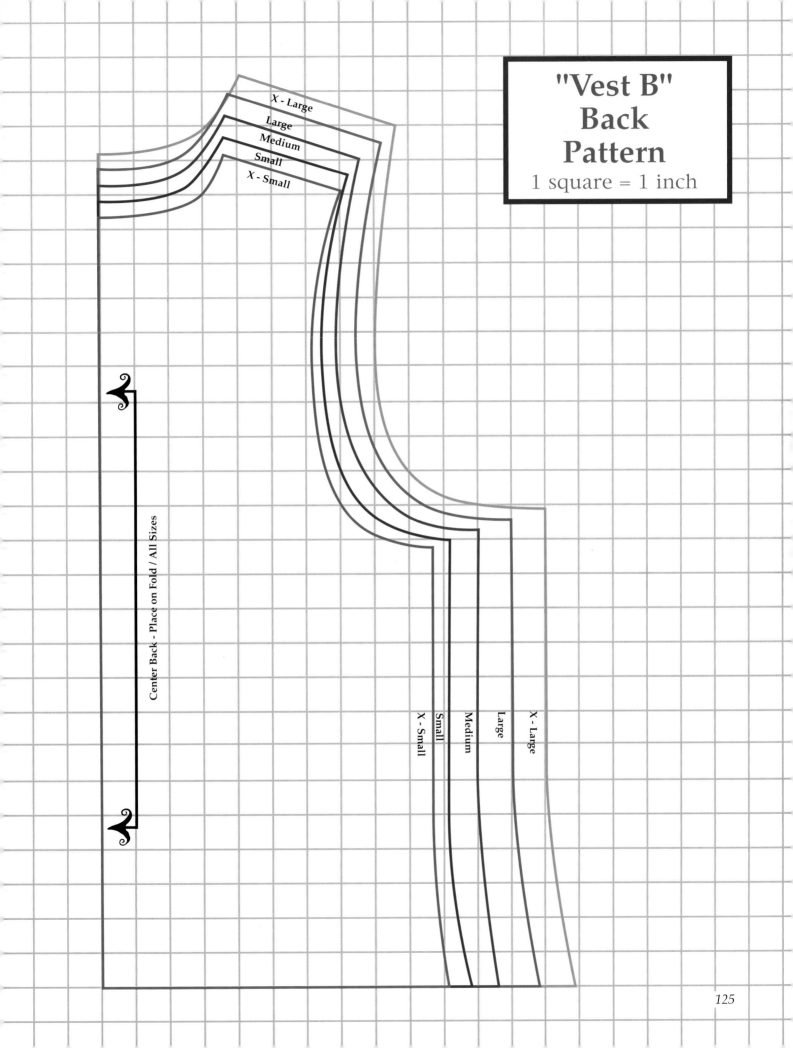

"Vest B"
Back
Pattern
1 square = 1 inch

X - Large
Large
Medium
Small
X - Small

Center Back - Place on Fold / All Sizes

X - Small
Small
Medium
Large
X - Large

125

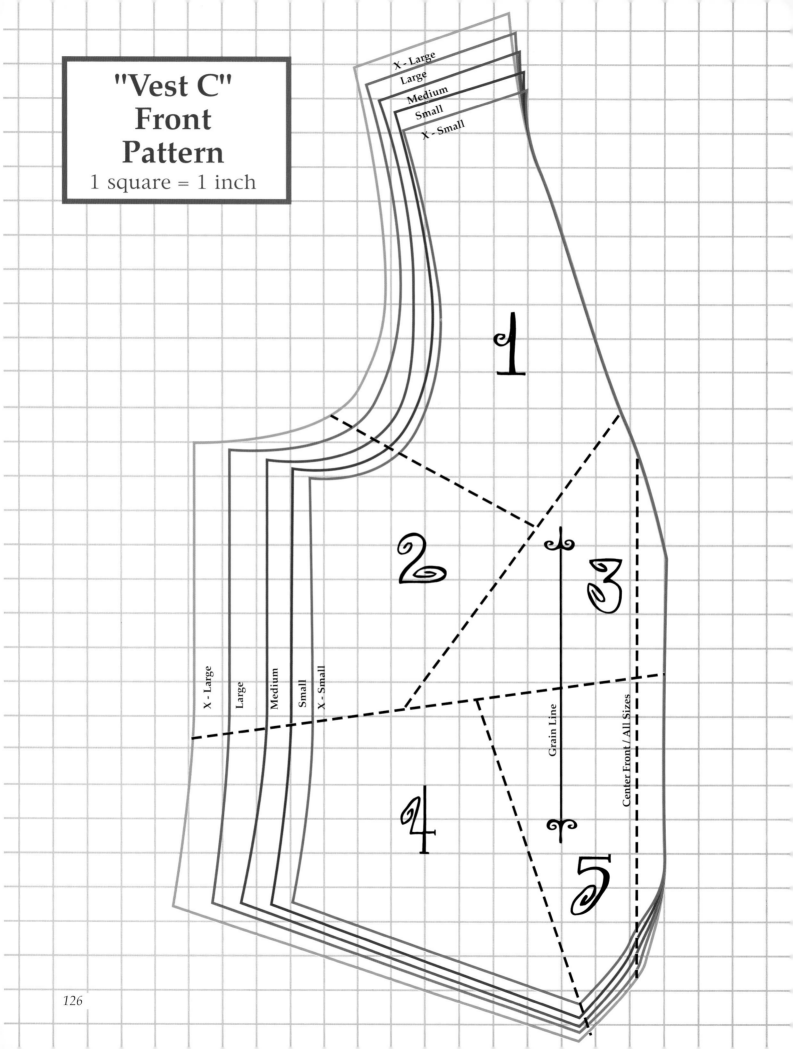

"Vest C"
Front
Pattern
1 square = 1 inch

X - Large
Large
Medium
Small
X - Small

1

2

3

X - Large
Large
Medium
Small
X - Small

Grain Line

Center Front / All Sizes

4

5

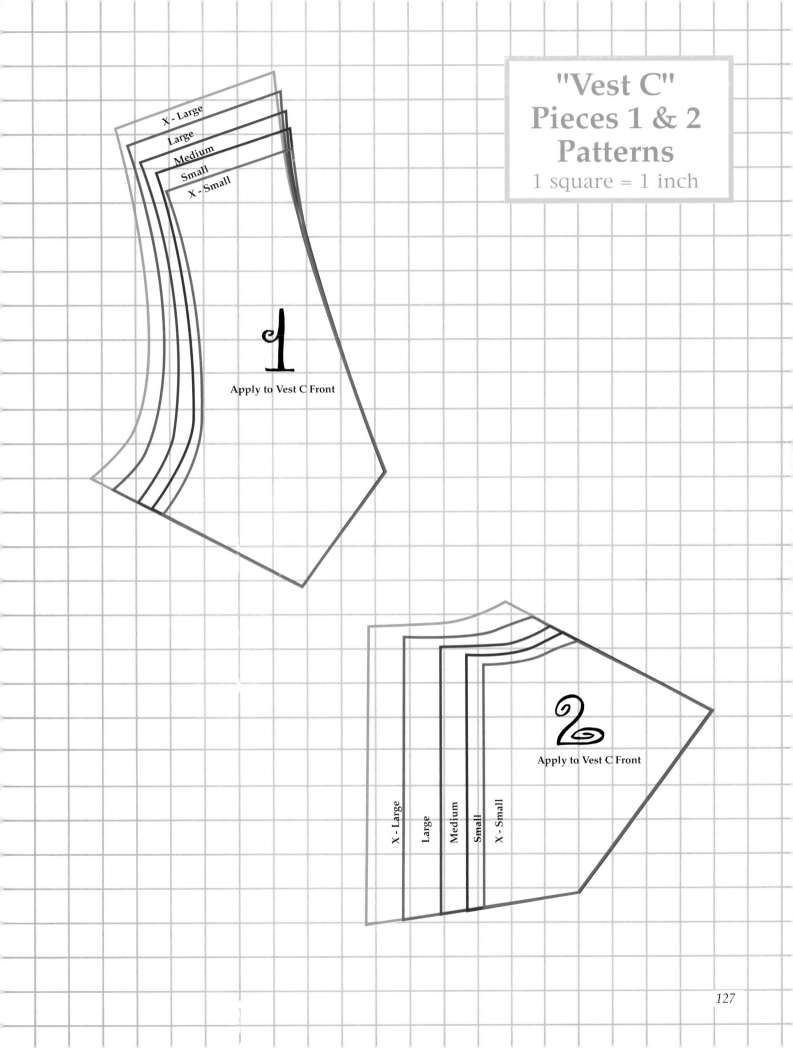

"Vest C"
Pieces 1 & 2
Patterns
1 square = 1 inch

X - Large
Large
Medium
Small
X - Small

1
Apply to Vest C Front

2
Apply to Vest C Front

X - Large
Large
Medium
Small
X - Small

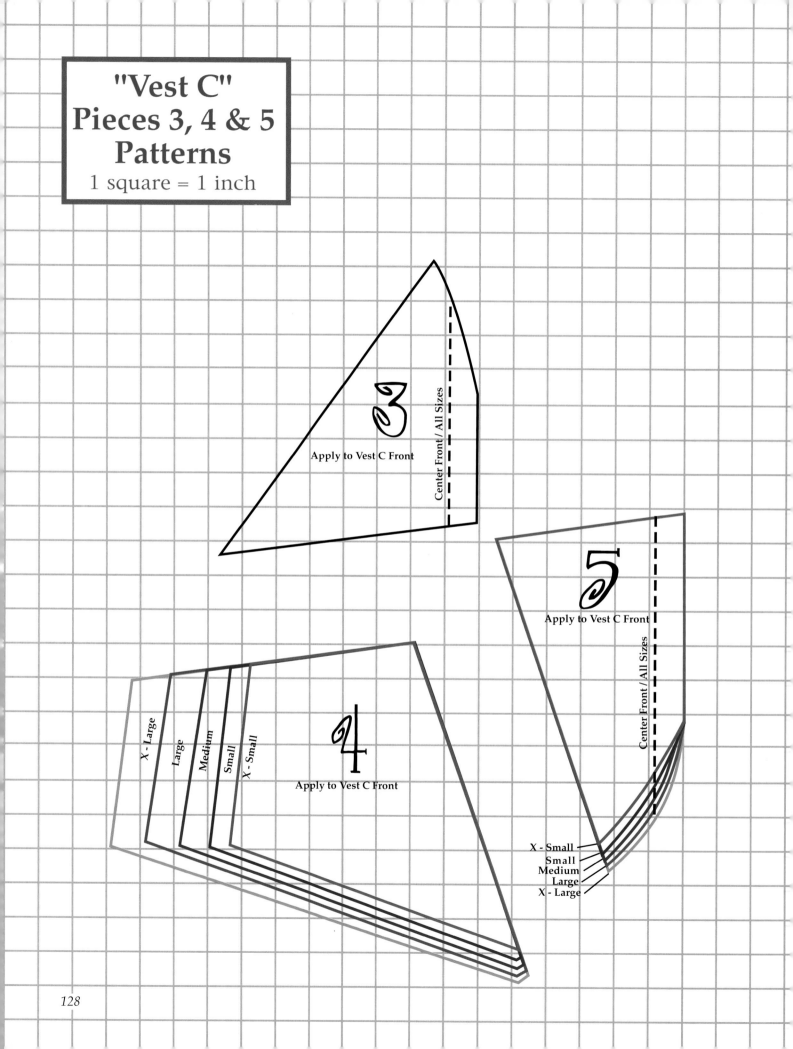

"Vest C"
Pieces 3, 4 & 5
Patterns
1 square = 1 inch

3
Apply to Vest C Front
Center Front / All Sizes

5
Apply to Vest C Front
Center Front / All Sizes

4
Apply to Vest C Front

X - Large
Large
Medium
Small
X - Small

X - Small
Small
Medium
Large
X - Large

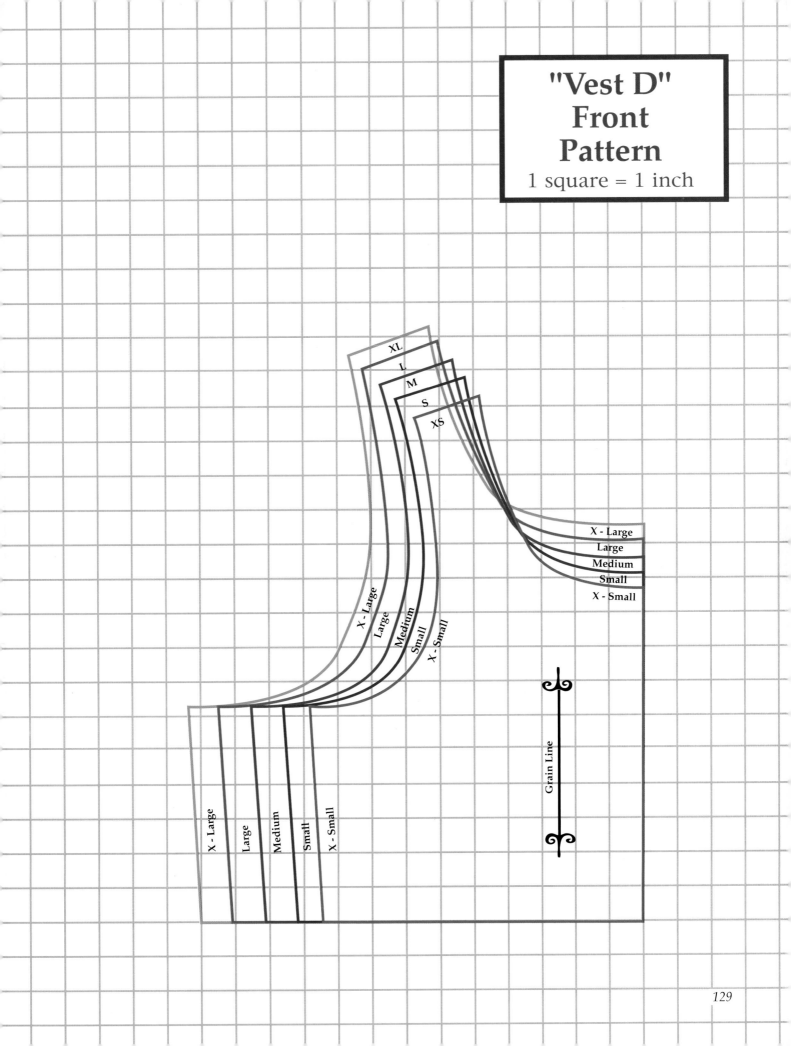

"Vest D"
Front
Pattern
1 square = 1 inch

XL
L
M
S
XS

X - Large
Large
Medium
Small
X - Small

X - Large
Large
Medium
Small
X - Small

Grain Line

X - Large
Large
Medium
Small
X - Small

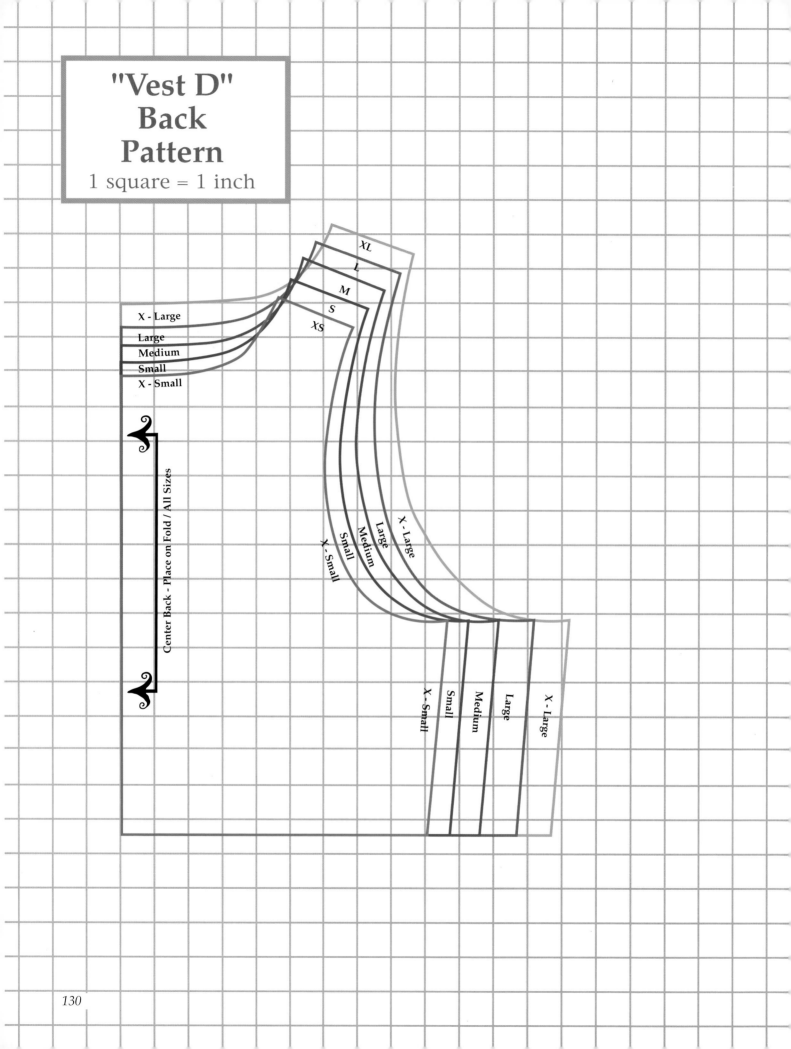

"Vest D"
Back
Pattern
1 square = 1 inch

XL
L
M
S
XS

X - Large
Large
Medium
Small
X - Small

Center Back - Place on Fold / All Sizes

X - Small
Small
Medium
Large
X - Large

X - Small
Small
Medium
Large
X - Large

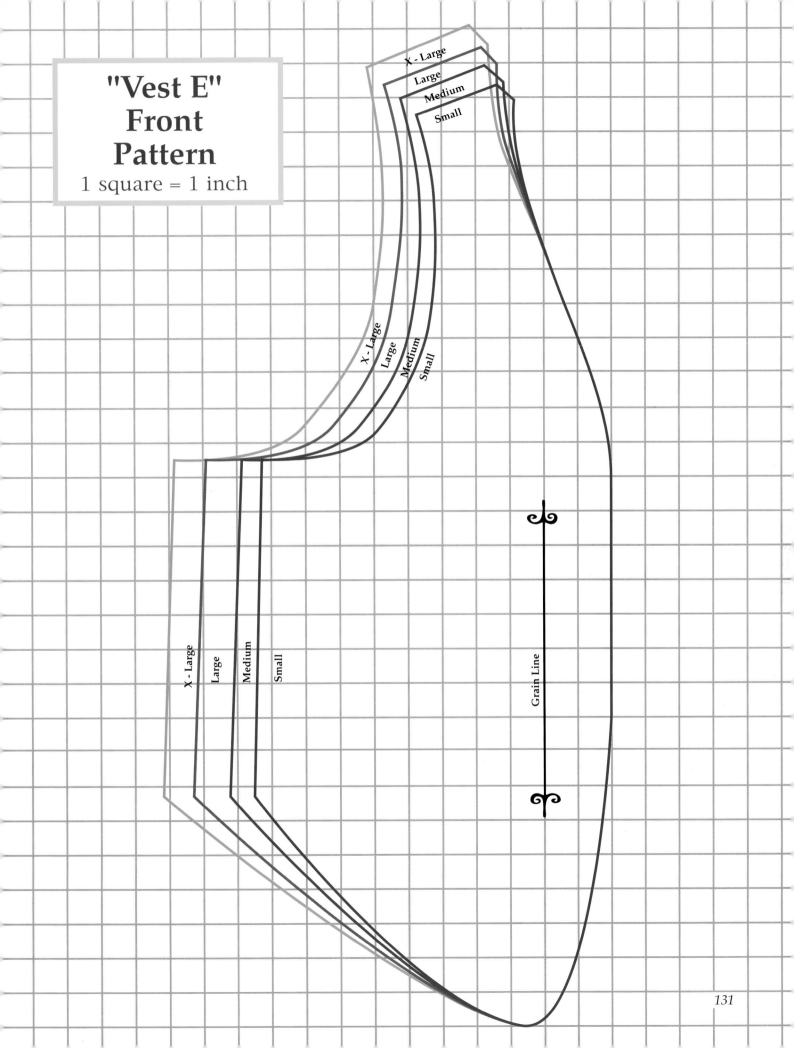

"Vest E"
Front
Pattern
1 square = 1 inch

X - Large
Large
Medium
Small

X - Large
Large
Medium
Small

X - Large
Large
Medium
Small

Grain Line

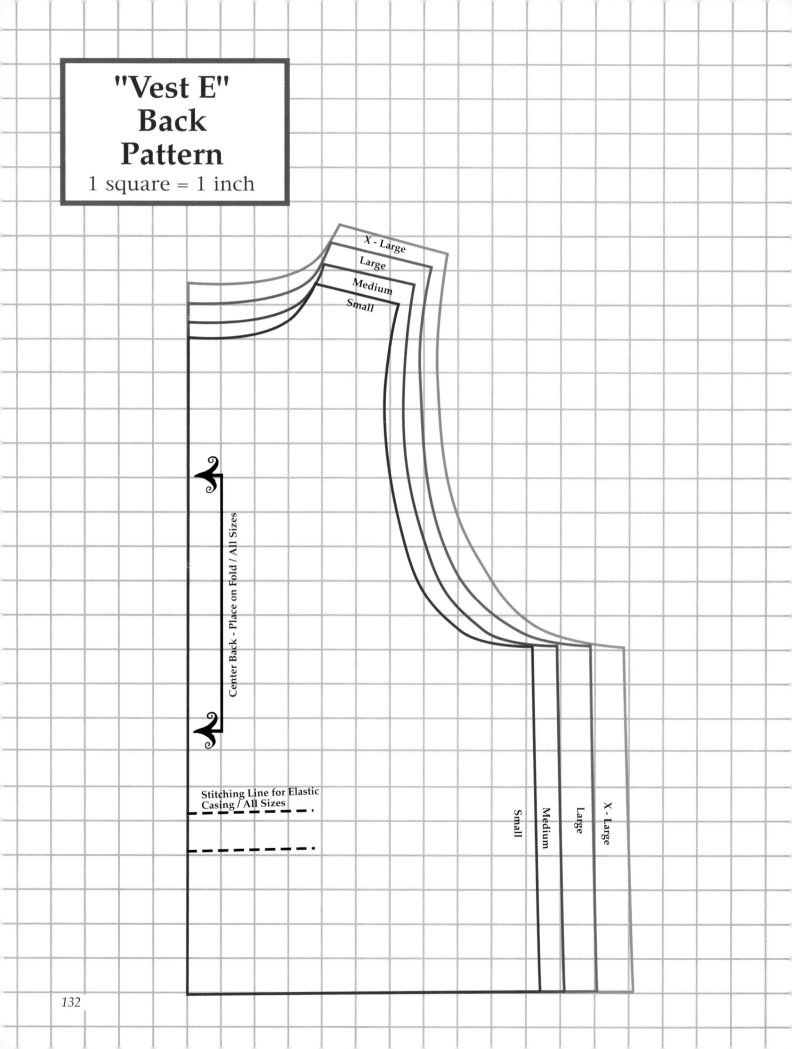

**"Vest E"
Back
Pattern**

1 square = 1 inch

X - Large

Large

Medium

Small

Center Back - Place on Fold / All Sizes

Stitching Line for Elastic
Casing / All Sizes

Small

Medium

Large

X - Large

132

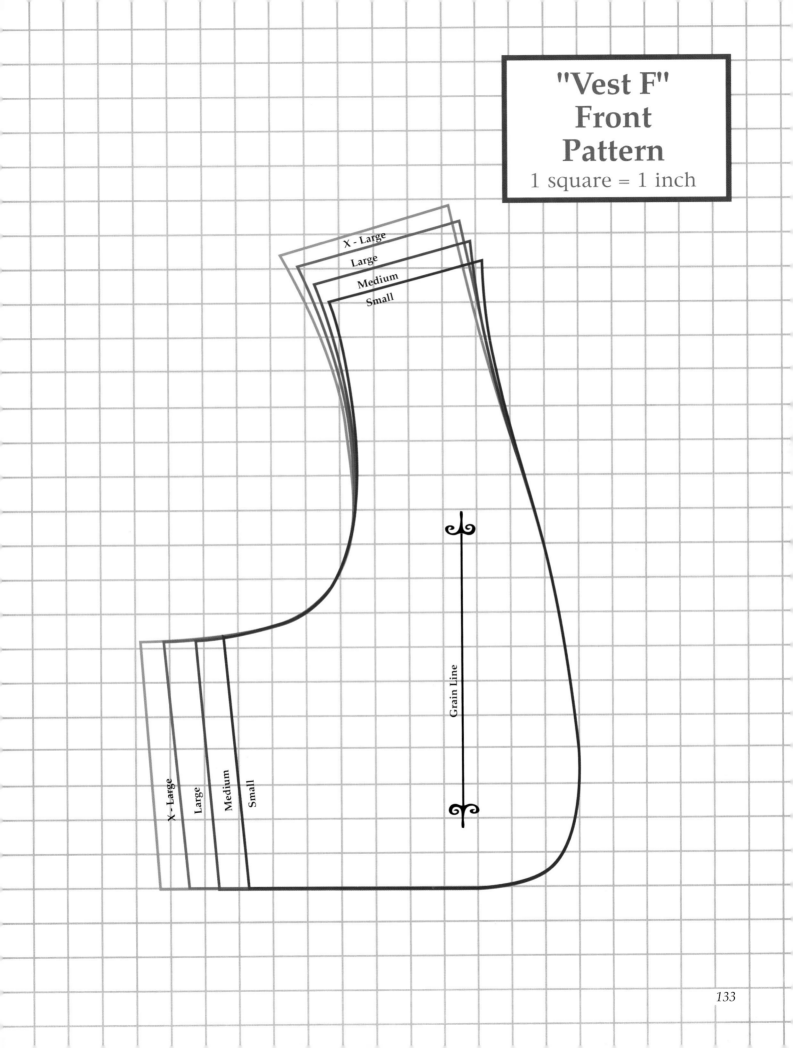

"Vest F"
Front
Pattern
1 square = 1 inch

X - Large
Large
Medium
Small

X - Large
Large
Medium
Small

Grain Line

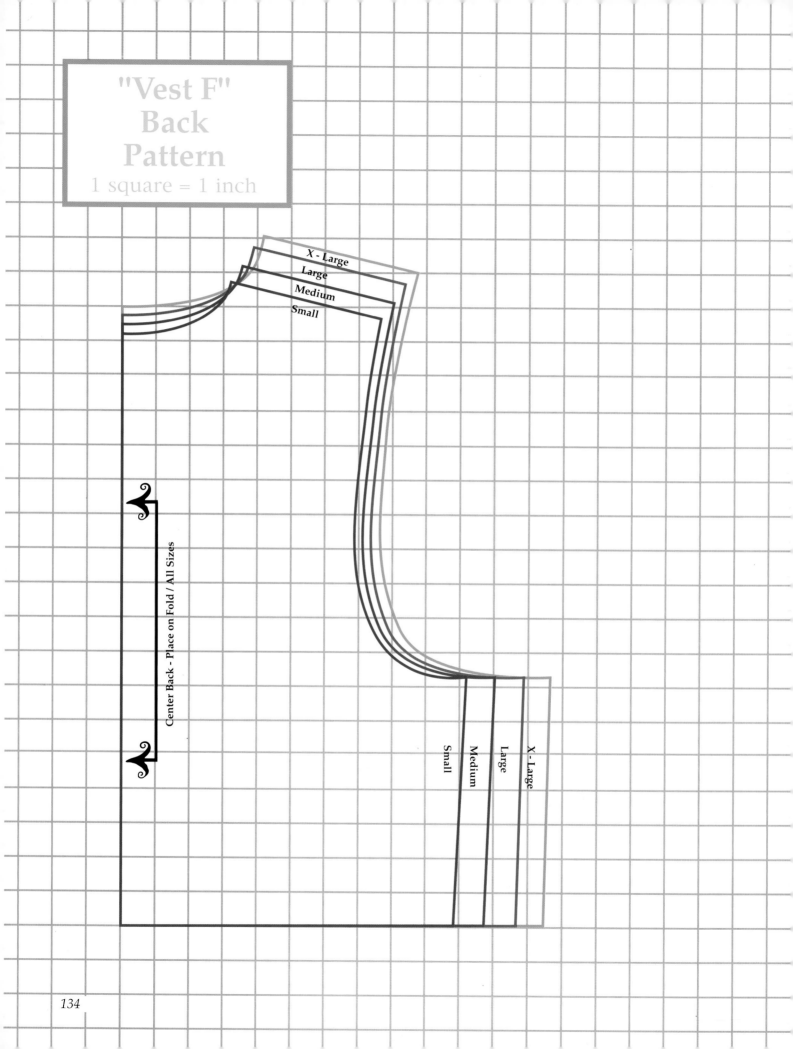

"Vest F"
Back
Pattern
1 square = 1 inch

X - Large
Large
Medium
Small

Center Back - Place on Fold / All Sizes

Small
Medium
Large
X - Large

134

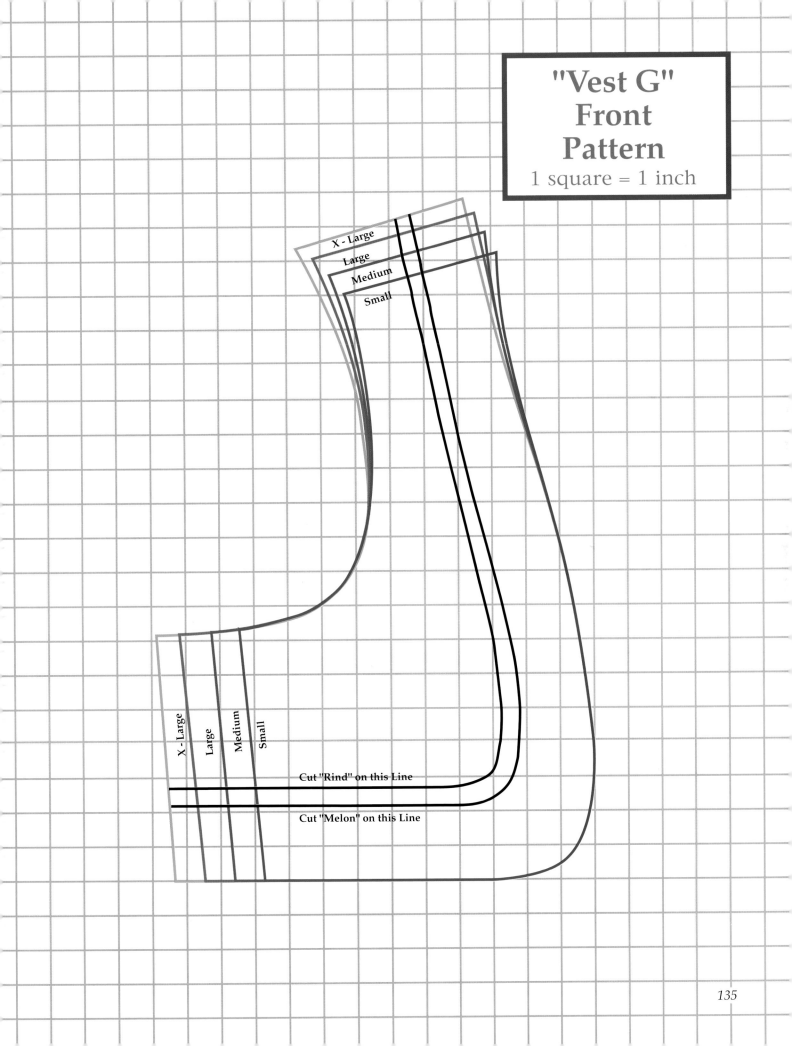

"Vest G"
Front
Pattern
1 square = 1 inch

X - Large
Large
Medium
Small

X - Large
Large
Medium
Small

Cut "Rind" on this Line

Cut "Melon" on this Line

135

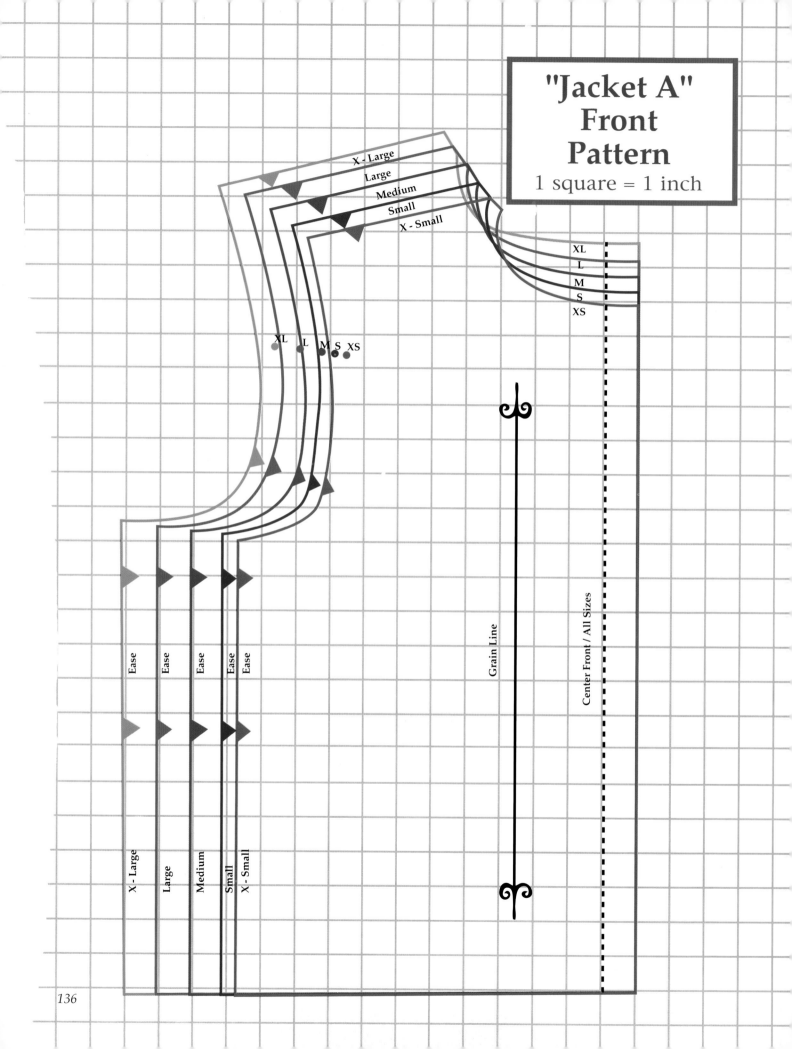

"Jacket A"
Front
Pattern
1 square = 1 inch

X - Large
Large
Medium
Small
X - Small

XL
L
M
S
XS

XL L M S XS

Grain Line

Center Front / All Sizes

Ease
Ease
Ease
Ease
Ease

X - Large
Large
Medium
Small
X - Small

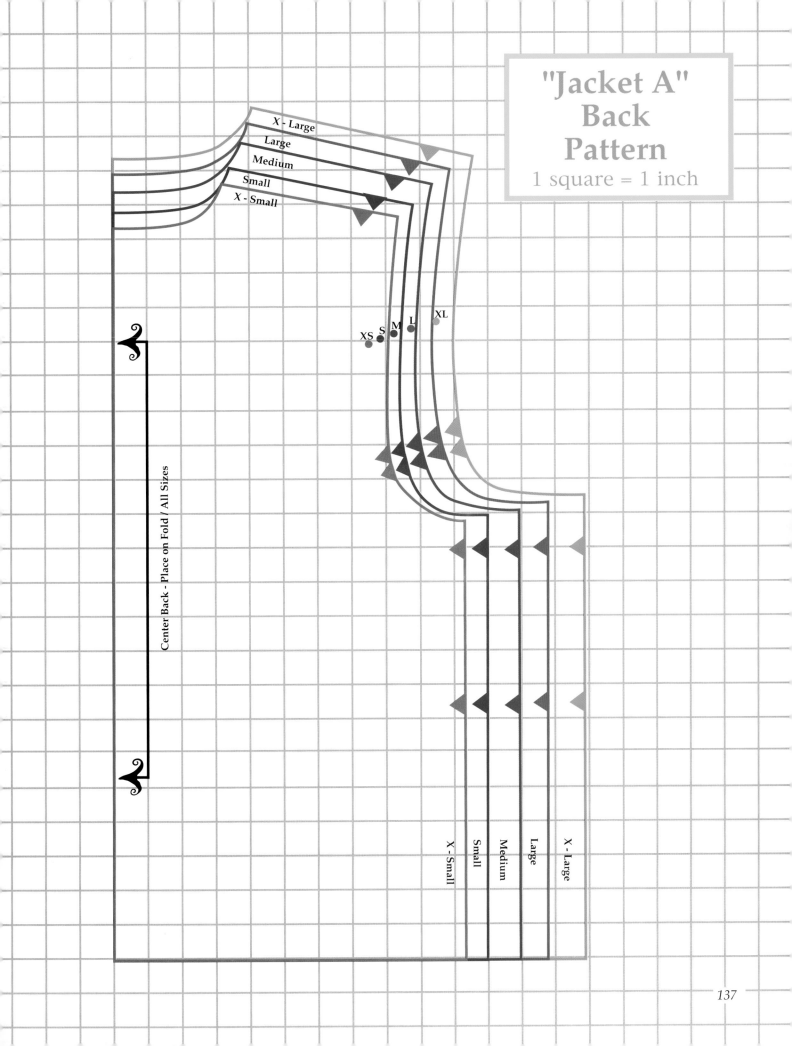

"Jacket A"
Back
Pattern
1 square = 1 inch

X - Large
Large
Medium
Small
X - Small

XS S M L XL

Center Back - Place on Fold / All Sizes

X - Small
Small
Medium
Large
X - Large

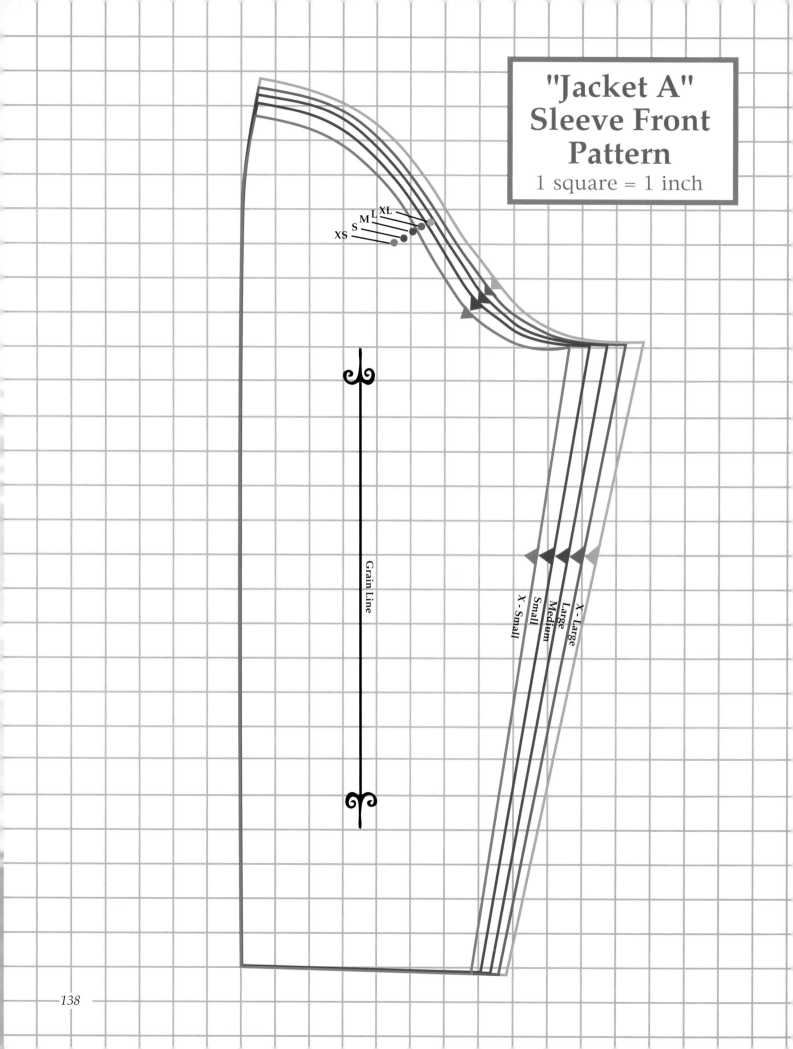

"Jacket A"
Sleeve Front
Pattern
1 square = 1 inch

XL
L
M
S
XS

Grain Line

X - Large
Large
Medium
Small
X - Small

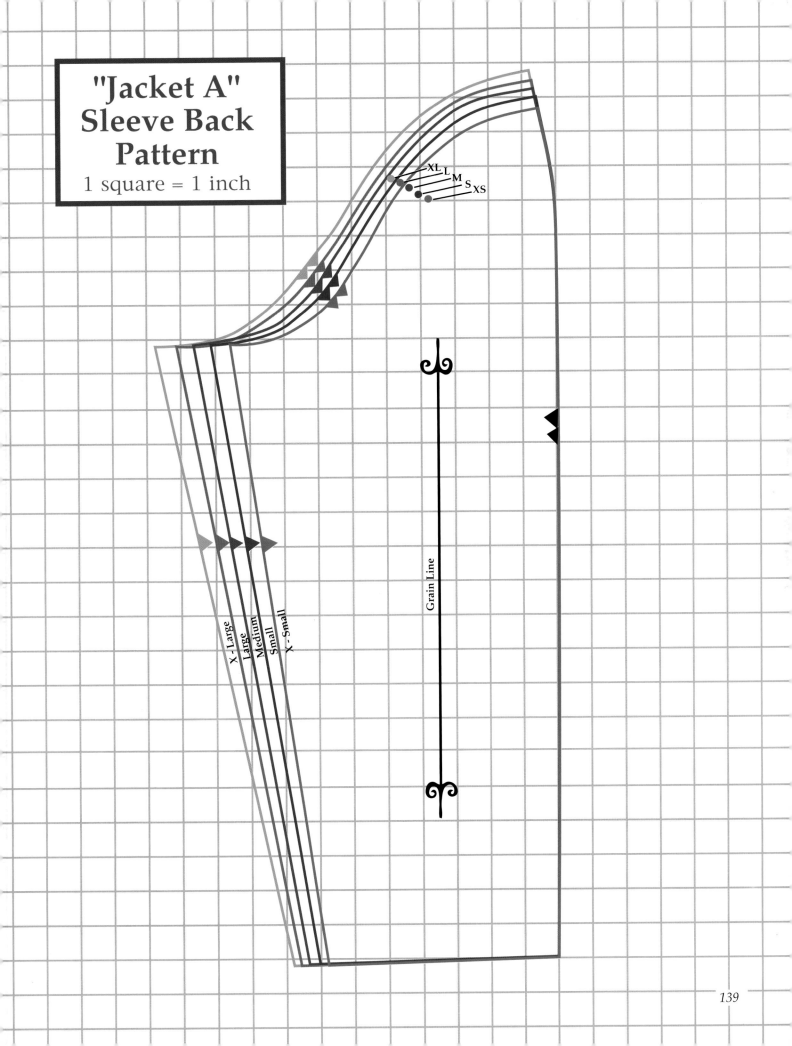

"Jacket A"
Sleeve Back
Pattern
1 square = 1 inch

XL
L
M
S
XS

X - Large
Large
Medium
Small
X - Small

Grain Line

139

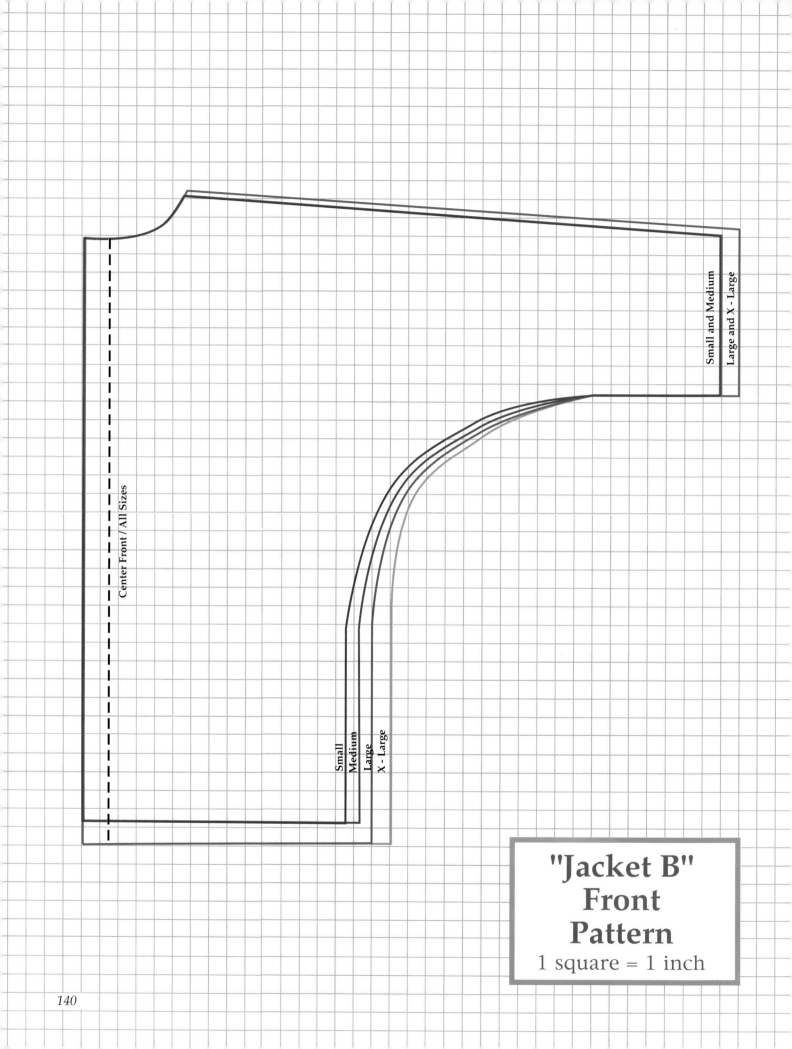

Center Front / All Sizes

Small and Medium

Large and X - Large

Small
Medium
Large
X - Large

"Jacket B"
Front
Pattern
1 square = 1 inch

140

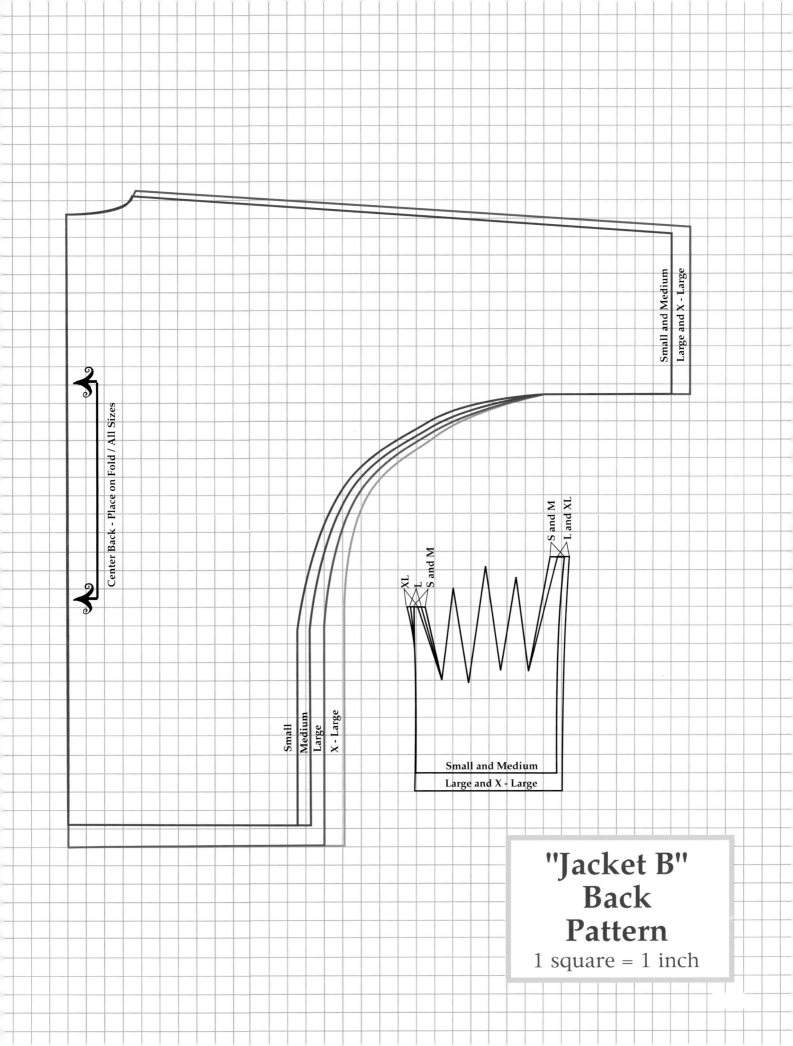

Center Back - Place on Fold / All Sizes

Small and Medium
Large and X - Large

Small
Medium
Large
X - Large

XL
L
S and M

S and M
L and XL

Small and Medium
Large and X - Large

"Jacket B"
Back
Pattern
1 square = 1 inch

METRIC CONVERSION CHART

MM-Millimetres   CM-Centimetres

INCHES TO MILLIMETRES AND CENTIMETRES

INCHES	MM	CM	INCHES	CM	INCHES	CM
1/8	3	0.9	9	22.9	30	76.2
1/4	6	0.6	10	25.4	31	78.7
3/8	10	1.0	11	27.9	32	81.3
1/2	13	1.3	12	30.5	33	83.8
5/8	16	1.6	13	33.0	34	86.4
3/4	19	1.9	14	35.6	35	88.9
7/8	22	2.2	15	38.1	36	91.4
1	25	2.5	16	40.6	37	94.0
1 1/4	32	3.2	17	43.2	38	96.5
1 1/2	38	3.8	18	45.7	39	99.1
1 3/4	44	4.4	19	48.3	40	101.6
2	51	5.1	20	50.8	41	104.1
2 1/2	64	6.4	21	53.3	42	106.7
3	76	7.6	22	55.9	43	109.2
3 1/2	89	8.9	23	58.4	44	111.8
4	102	10.2	24	61.0	45	114.3
4 1/2	114	11.4	25	63.5	46	116.8
5	127	12.7	26	66.0	47	119.4
6	152	15.2	27	68.6	48	121.9
7	178	17.8	28	71.1	49	124.5
8	203	20.3	29	73.7	50	127.0

YARDS TO METRES

YARDS	METRES	YARDS	METRES	YARDS	METRES	YARDS	METRES	YARDS	METRES
1/8	0.11	2 1/8	1.94	4 1/8	3.77	6 1/8	5.60	8 1/8	7.43
1/4	0.23	2 1/4	2.06	4 1/4	3.89	6 1/4	5.72	8 1/4	7.54
3/8	0.34	2 3/8	2.17	4 3/8	4.00	6 3/8	5.83	8 3/8	7.66
1/2	0.46	2 1/2	2.29	4 1/2	4.11	6 1/2	5.94	8 1/2	7.77
5/8	0.57	2 5/8	2.40	4 5/8	4.23	6 5/8	6.06	8 5/8	7.89
3/4	0.69	2 3/4	2.51	4 3/4	4.34	6 3/4	6.17	8 3/4	8.00
7/8	0.80	2 7/8	2.63	4 7/8	4.46	6 7/8	6.29	8 7/8	8.12
1	0.91	3	2.74	5	4.57	7	6.40	9	8.23
1 1/8	1.03	3 1/8	2.86	5 1/8	4.69	7 1/8	6.52	9 1/8	8.34
1 1/4	1.14	3 1/4	2.97	5 1/4	4.80	7 1/4	6.63	9 1/4	8.46
1 3/8	1.26	3 3/8	3.09	5 3/8	4.91	7 3/8	6.74	9 3/8	8.57
1 1/2	1.37	3 1/2	3.20	5 1/2	5.03	7 1/2	6.86	9 1/2	8.69
1 5/8	1.49	3 5/8	3.31	5 5/8	5.14	7 5/8	6.97	9 5/8	8.80
1 3/4	1.60	3 3/4	3.43	5 3/4	5.26	7 3/4	7.09	9 3/4	8.92
1 7/8	1.71	3 7/8	3.54	5 7/8	5.37	7 7/8	7.20	9 7/8	9.03
2	1.83	4	3.66	6	5.49	8	7.32	10	9.14

INDEX

ABOUT THE AUTHOR

PATRICK LOSE has spent his professional years in a variety of creative fields. He began his career as a costume designer for stage and screen. Costume credits include more than 50 productions and include work with celebrities such as Liza Minnelli and Jane Seymour.

An artist and illustrator since childhood, Patrick works in many mediums. When he sits down to "doodle" at the drawing board, he never knows what one of his designs might become. Whether it's a cross-stitch piece, wearable art, a greeting card, an ornament, or a piece of furniture, he enjoys creating it all.

His crafts, clothing, and home decorating accessories have appeared frequently in national magazines including *Better Homes and Gardens*, *Country Crafts*, *Christmas Ideas*, *Halloween Tricks and Treats*, *Folk Art Christmas*, *Santa Claus*, *Decorative Woodcrafts*, *Craft and Wear*, and *American Patchwork and Quilting*. Publications featuring his designs have reached over 18 million subscribers.

Patrick also designs fabrics for United Notions and Fabrics, many of which were used to create the jackets and vests featured throughout this book.

OUT ON A WHIM, Patrick's company name, appropriately describes his original creations. Available in fabric and crafts stores nationwide, his patterns for making clothing, dolls, home decorating accessories, and holiday crafts feature folk-art whimsy with a contemporary twist.